W9-CAT-955

The Skipping Stone

John Fodale, Dcn

authorHOUSE®

AuthorHouse™
1663 Liberty Drive, Suite 200
Bloomington, IN 47403
www.authorhouse.com
Phone: 1-800-839-8640

© 2009 John Fodale. All rights reserved.

No part of this book may be reproduced, stored in a retrieval system, or transmitted by any means without the written permission of the author.

First published by AuthorHouse 1/6/2009

ISBN: 978-1-4389-2100-6 (sc)
ISBN: 978-1-4389-2099-3 (hc)

Printed in the United States of America
Bloomington, Indiana

This book is printed on acid-free paper.

This book is dedicated to
my wife Hannah and our three children
John Jr, Edward and Lynn

Appreciation

Special thanks to Linda DeRosa my good friend who edited and formatted my first draft and did the art work for the cover. I also am very grateful to Paula Malloy who did the final edit and reviewed the content for spiritual value.

Contents

Acknowledgments 161

Forward

This paper was originally written as a guide for my children to follow when I am not here to help them. It is meant to give them the basic tools to help them get back on track during difficult times. Although this was written for my children, I realize that this could be used by others when they need encouragement or direction in life.

What I have written is food for the body, mind and soul. The contents may lean toward the spiritual at times, because when you enter into depth in your life you find your soul and its creator; in doing that you find yourself and your purpose.

This writing is helpful for people of all faiths, because when I speak of God, I speak of the God and Father of all people of all faiths. We are all spiritual people, but the way we express our spirituality is through our religion. No matter how you worship or what religion you follow, it is all the same God.

I have used what is written here in the workplace over a fifteen-year period and it has helped sales reps gain a deeper understanding of their clients and their businesses. This translates into better relationships and a greater cash flow for both, as well as a greater satisfaction in the work place. This method has also been used in private sessions in the work place and in counseling environments at my parish. All of the following information has been used in several environments including a series of spiritual talks. What is written in this book can benefit a person's soul and restore order and balance in life. So, I ask you to be open to what you read. Use it based on how you are inspired and you will profit from it.

Reflection

The message of this book is depth. Depth causes us to reflect on our lives and when we reflect on where we have been or where we are going, we grow in all of the virtues, especially wisdom. But depth is not easy to pass on to others, even if it will help others to understand their lives a little better and make their path a little smoother. One of the things I have noticed as I have gotten older is younger people think I know less now than I did a few years ago. It is as though they think that each morning I get out of bed, I have lost some important brain cells. I tend to simplify things, so they think that I can't change with the future. This is not true because the things of great value that we can pass on are the simple things in life. These do not change over time and will help them use the new and wonderful information they have gained in a better way.

The thing we bring to the table when we get older is wisdom; better known as common sense or horse sense. It is the foundation of all knowledge that we place in our minds. Notice, I used the word place in our minds rather then fill our minds. To be educated properly we place information in our minds, so that it fits together, with all of the other knowledge we have gained. It creates a better foundation from which we must make important decisions.

Reflection is one of the most important tools you can have to enter into depth. It allows you to understand how you arrived at the point you are. As you reflect back, you may put some things down and pick up others. By reflecting back in life while doing some deep thinking you will sort things out and as you begin to understand how you arrived where you are; you will live a deeper more meaningful life with confidence, good character and peace.

When I first reflected back into my life, I realized that I was able to point to a few events that formed me into the person I am today. Reflection taught me how to separate my true self from the self my parents wanted me to be, or the person others thought I should be.

It is always good to begin your reflection remembering the point in life you are at today. So I begin with, I am 65 years old and am semi-retired. I also have just celebrated my 11th year as a deacon of the Roman Catholic Church. As I look back over the years, I understand that I am not the most educated person that you have met. In my 65 years, I have been a good father and at times a bad father. I have been a good husband and a bad husband, a good family member and a bad one, a good son and also a bad son. To sum it up, I am an average person who has made his share of mistakes. I look at everyday life in a simplistic way with peace clarity and order. That doesn't mean I don't have down days. It just means I understand them better and can see most of them coming.

Transformation can happen to anyone no matter where they are in life. All you need is the will to detach yourself from your current way of life and have a little patience and perseverance. Most of all you must trust in God.

I discovered in the first thirty five years of my life that I lived in a "choppy" existence. Then one day I woke up and I began to understand that I was not my parents and didn't have to live like them. I began to claim my own identity. I came to understand that I was most happy serving others in each situation that came to me. I learned that in serving others I was using their education. They would ask me to do something based on their knowledge and I would respond and learn. The more I became a servant the more I learned.

I learned that I am most content serving others, helping them to be successful and in that I learned that in their success I had success. So that's who I am. Now at some point in life each person must take some time and reflect on who they are. How they were raised and separate out those pieces that are theirs and those pieces that others put there to help them grow or raise them. It is at this point that a person can begin to realize who they are.

Because of my upbringing I always learned things through experience and I always had a simple approach to all things I accomplished. Because of the simple view of things I used to be called on to look at a situation and be able to help people see more clearly. I would be invited to a meeting or to counsel a person and where the simple answer was hidden from them, I was able to point out how to overcome a roadblock that may have been stopping them.

In the rear of the book I have placed some of my homilies that give a simple approach to helping a person to have clear insight to get through most situations in life. I hope as you read this you will find out how to appreciate what you have, as well as appreciate all that comes your way. You will also find that there is a lesson to be learned in everything if you pay attention and if you do you will become more attentive and considerate to others as you grow.

The message

A few years ago I was thinking back to when I was a little boy playing by a pond. I would look for stones, which I would try to throw and slide across the pond to the other side by skipping them on the top of the water. As I thought of this skipping stone I realized that if the stone didn't stop and sink into the water it would never become part of the pond. It would have an existence of length and width but never any depth. I realized that I was just like the skipping stone. I was living a two dimensional life, a life with no depth.

I would go to work in the morning and I would have casual conversations with people. I would have the same with my family. All I could see was the end goal in each thing I did. I would look at the clock to get to five pm. Then I would look at the clock again to see how long it would take to get home. Then I looked at the clock to see when I could finish dinner and then how long before I go to bed. I saw no depth; only watching the goal like the stone. Just trying to get to the destination, and always missing the enjoyment of what I was doing. In doing this I missed my children's younger years, lots of my relationship with my wife and other friends in my life.

I had so much to do. I was goal oriented and being goal oriented makes you thirst for closure in each thing you do. It breeds impatience. To have goals is good but not if they control your life and hold you back from enjoying what you are doing in depth. But in my blindness I allowed my goals to control my life so that I never really paid attention to all of the beautiful things I had in my life and all of the beautiful people that were around me. General Electric had a motto "Progress Is our most important product." I seemed to be living that motto and that was my mistake. The motto was okay for G.E., but not for a person who wants to live a full life; enjoying their children, work and people God has placed in their lives.

Depth brings life

So, how do we find this thing called depth? It's easy, just slow down. A few years ago I went to lunch with a friend of mine who was upset about something that happened to him at work. We went to a restaurant in a shopping center. I remember it was a warm sunny day in July. My friend was so upset that all he did at lunch was talk about the problem he had because that's all he could see in front of him.

During lunch I wasn't able to say much. When lunch was over and we went out to the parking lot I said to my friend, "Would you do me a favor?" He said, "Sure." I said, "This may sound unusual but would you walk ten steps with me?" He said, "OK." Then I said, "But before you do tell me what you see." He said, "I see a parking lot." Tell me more I said. He said, in a hurried way "I see cars." I said, "Tell me more." He said, "I see people." More I said. He finally began to recognize the color of the cars and the way people were dressed.

When he was done I said, "Now let's take the ten steps." He began to walk quickly and I grabbed him by the shoulder and said, "Do them with me at my pace." I took one deliberate step slow enough that you would feel your foot in your shoe as you placed it on the ground. Then we took another step slowly then another until we took the ten steps. I said to him, "Now how do you feel?" He said, "Peaceful." Then I asked him what he saw once more and he said, "I see the same things as I did before." I asked if anything was different and he said, "Yes. Before as I looked at the parking lot it was like looking at television, and I didn't feel part of it now I feel part of what I see."

Like the skipping stone that stopped and entered into the depth of the lake and became part of it, so too did my friend who slowed down and became part of life. We at times are like the skipping stone in life and until we slow down, we will not become part of life or understand it. We will just see life in two dimensions without depth.

Another example of moving into depth is if you imagine yourself driving on a highway and you are exceeding the speed limit. But because of your speed all you can see are white lines and bumpers. But when you slow down to the speed limit you begin to see the trees and the grass along the highway. Your view widens and you have moved into depth. When you enter into depth in your life you will be able to better understand people, your work projects and yourself in a way that you never did before. When you understand these things you truly begin making real progress. So slow down and find your life.

Becoming part of life

Most people try to conquer life not become one with it. They feel that they must lead or control all of the time or they are not happy or doing their job. Picture yourself dancing with someone and the both of you are trying to lead. The first things you will notice is that you are always fighting the motions of the other person. When you do this you don't hear the music and you end up looking foolish and out of step. This attitude destroys projects and relationships. To live life you need to give yourself up to the music of life and only lead when called upon. As the great mystics would say life is a dance and we are the dancers. God is our partner and God leads most of the time.

Becoming one with what you are doing or your choices is very important because it is the first step in learning how to live a full and appreciative life. A few years ago there were some athletes who went to Nepal with the Peace Corp. Each day they worked with the people using their strength and youth to make better conditions for the town's people.

One day they were asked to participate in one of the festivals the town celebrated in which the town's people would climb the mountain on the outskirts of the village. All of the people would participate in the climb to the top. There would be men and women of all ages as well as children that would make the climb. The athletes agreed to participate. It looked easy to them. It was just a spiral walk up the mountain. They were young; what did they have to lose.

On the morning of the walk they slept a little later than usual because they felt it to be an easy task. They set off and in the first hour they moved ahead of most of the town's people. They passed men, women, children and those who walked with canes to assist them. In the second hour they had a commanding lead over the whole town. They were getting a little tired so they decided to take a rest. As they sat on the side of the road the town's people began to catch up so they were off again. About two thirds of the way up the hill they stopped again, but this time they were too tired to go on. They watched the men; women and children pass them by. They even saw women with children being carried on their backs pass them, as well as those with canes.

Exhausted they went back to the village and went to sleep. When they awoke they heard the music and dancing of the celebration. They went to the feast and saw the chief asked if all of the villagers made the climb. To their surprise he said yes; every last one of them made the climb. Then he paused and said except for your group.

They said to the chief that they didn't understand how everyone could make it and we couldn't. The chief said, "The answer is simple. You tried to conquer the mountain, where as they became one with the mountain. For them it was a religious experience for you, only conquering".

As you live your life you must try to become one with "it", you should not try to conquer "it". It is the same with the small things in life that are before us. Like our families, friendships and projects and even God, becoming one with them brings life and peace. Trying to conquer them brings anxiety and disappointment.

The need to find the quiet place within you

To become one with what you do takes a little time and a little understanding of how we as human beings are put together. People are made up of three things: body, mind and spirit or soul. These three parts move at different speeds and have different interests. The body will always want to take the easy way of living, the mind will always try to figure things out even when there is nothing to figure out and the Spirit wants only to guide and be at peace.

These three, as I said, move at different speeds. As the day goes on they grow miles apart. The mind is pulling one-way and the body another and the spirit still another. So it becomes your job to bring them back to a starting point, so they can begin again. When the body, mind and spirit of a person are in tune and working together you will never be more powerful in what you are doing. Getting these three in order is called finding your center. It is not meditation there is no thinking involved and no repetition is needed.

To understand how this centering works picture your mind in three parts. The first is the largest of the three and it is where most of the conscious activity happens. The second is next largest and it is where you live. The third is the smallest where your center is.

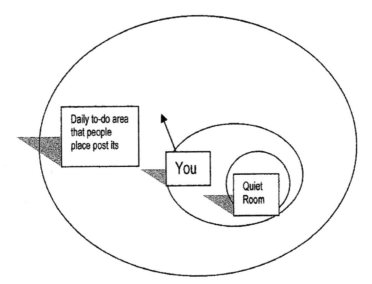

In our normal state we face the large part of the mind and in this large part all of the current thoughts are present. As you go through your day you place little post-its in your mind like the things you have to do today and in the future. Some of the things you place there are yours and some are placed there by others. Some of the things are real and some are imagined.

My wife may ask me to fix the stove this week, pick up milk on the way home. My manager may say I need a report completed by the end of the month. My children may be asking for some time to work or play with them. As you can see the accumulation of these thoughts and caring for them becomes work, and a little confusing at times. Sometimes they lose their priority and we never get them done. They just sit there waiting, producing guilt or excuses as to why we didn't do them

Now, all day long I, being in the second part of the mind, am looking out at all of these things and I continue to poll them to make sure I don't forget anything. Should something begin to fade away I bring it back to life by thinking about it by giving it my time and attention. Some of the things in there may not be nice, like the thought of being angry with someone.

The way to find your center is by turning away from all of this confusion. Face the smallest part of the mind which is a quiet place, you might call it a secret room. When go to this secret place for a short period of time, all of the things you have been holding on to disappear. Only those tasks that are important remain there when you turn back. It's like emptying a recycle bin on a computer. When you find your center all of the chains, cords and attachments that keep you from being peaceful or calm are broken. When you come back you are peaceful and your body, mind and spirit are in harmony moving in the same direction and speed, doing one thing at a time. When you do this you have depth in your actions, you begin to have life.

Entering the quiet place

The process that I use to bring people to that quiet room within them is the following:

1.   First find a chair that is comfortable for you and then sit in a position that is relaxing to you.

2.   Close your eyes and take a deep breath in through the nose and hold it for a second or two. Let it out slowly from the mouth. This is done three times. As you do this you will begin to feel relaxed and feel the anxiety being released through your legs and arms.

3.   Then bring your attention to your shoulders and you feel the cloth touching your skin. Be attentive to that for a short period of time.

4.   Then move down and be aware of your stomach and how the cloth of your shirt touches your skin as you breathe.

5.   Then move down and be aware of how your legs are touching the seat.

6.   Continue on and be attentive as to how your knees are bent.

7.   Then move your attention to your feet and feel the leather or cloth of your shoe touching your foot. Be aware of your toes each one separately, and move them.

8.   Then move your attention to the top of your head and stay there for a moment.

9.   Then move down and feel your eyes and how they touch the back of your eyelids.

10. Moved down further and feel the air passing over your sinuses as you breathe.

11. Once more move and feel your tongue as it touches your teeth.

12. Then finally move back to the shoulders and feel the cloth as it touches your skin and then continue on your own for as long as you feel the peacefulness.

When you return

When you return, open your eyes slowly and become familiar with your surroundings again. Don't try to move back into your life too quickly or you may become irritable because you haven't given yourself enough time to adjust.

Look at your watch and you will see that 15 to 20 minutes has passed. You'll find it difficult to speak because of the peacefulness that you feel. You'll find no thoughts in your mind and no anxiety. You'll be able to focus now on whatever you choose to do. You will become one with your work and it will have your full attention. You will go slower and get more done and what you do will be of great quality. When you speak with someone you will be a better listener and you will know when to speak and when not to. You will think before you act or speak. If you're writing, the words will flow from you and you will not have writer's block. You'll find that things don't bother you as much as they did before, like the attitude of a person you work with, or a family member. Your feelings will change toward a person that might not have been to your liking. To your surprise their feelings may change towards you without you doing anything.

If you do this once a day you'll find your day will go peacefully. You'll have no anxiety and you'll enjoy your life more as well as your work, your family and your friends. As you practice this little exercise you will notice that the world is not changing you are. You will find that you are not fighting the world; you are becoming one with it.

Because life doesn't change, you will still have things come your way that can be a problem to you, but you will find that you handle them better. If you feel the anxiety beginning to come back just take a short break and go back to your center.

If you don't have time to do the centering exercises you will be able to find your center by placing your finger gently on the center of your chest and feel the cloth touch your skin. Almost instantly you will feel your arms, legs and whole body as the anxiety leaves you. Do this for a few moments before a meeting and you will restore the peacefulness and focus within you. You can also take a pencil and roll it in your fingers and as you feel the bumps this will bring you to your center. You could also take a slow walk, which will help you enter into the peacefulness. The goal is to leave the outside world for a short time and enter into yourself. Sit in the quiet so that the chains that hold you down can be detached and you will feel free.

Where you have been

Now it's time to tell you where you have been for these few minutes. When you turn into that small part of yourself you are paying a visit to the seat of your soul or another way to say it is that you have been sitting with your creator. In that small piece of time you gain confidence in yourself, trust in others and heal old wounds. You come out more mature and you know that you are loved. When you know that your creator loves and accepts you, you don't need anyone else to love you. When you feel loved, all you do is more focused, free and mature.

It's like this, picture yourself in a company and each day you think what you are doing is not enough and you can't seem to please anyone. You begin to hoard information and use your skills sparingly, so that you create a kind of job security. Then one day the Chairman of the Board of your company meets you in the hallway and he knows your name. He tells you how much he likes your work and he knows of your accomplishments. He then tells you that he wants you to be with the company for many years to come. In those few moments he takes away all of your fears, gives you confidence in yourself and abilities and reassures you that you have nothing to worry about in your future. After this meeting you are more relaxed and you are not afraid to share information or your skills with others. Going to this quiet place within your self is like meeting the chairman of the board of your life and soul.

Self Personal choices

There are very few things in life we control, but the things we do control are the things that build our character and place us on the path to peace, happiness and success.

The things we control are within us. We can control our attitude, our expectations and our respect for others. If we learn to control what is within ourselves we can truly change the world and the people we meet along the way.

What I have outlined in this section are the steps in learning who we are and how to attain acceptance and confidence in the person we are; so that we can create good long lasting relationships in our lives.

Remember that when you make this journey and enter into the depth of yourself you will be with the chairman of the board of your soul and to the chairman no one is ugly, stupid, unlovable or unaccepted.

Who are you?

There is an old story of a woman who was in a coma and was near death. She suddenly had a feeling that she was taken up to heaven and stood before the judgment seat of God. "Who are you?" A voice said to her. I'm the wife of the Mayor, she said. I didn't ask whose wife you are but who are you. I'm the mother of four children. I didn't ask whose mother you are but who are you. I'm a schoolteacher. I didn't ask what your profession is but who are you. And so it went. No matter what she replied she didn't seem to give a satisfactory answer to the question "who are you"? I'm a Christian she said. I didn't ask what your religion is but who are you. I'm the one who went to church every day and helped the poor and needy. I didn't ask what you did but who are you. She eventually failed the examination and was sent back to earth. When she recovered from her illness, she was determined to find out who she was so she could live the life she was meant to live.

To find out who we are, we need to sift through all of the things within us. We need to look at what we were like when we were children. We need to look at how we were raised and through our experiences what we liked and disliked. It's like a fisherman hauling in his net. He sits and decides what is of value and what is not. Sometimes our parents bestow upon us rules and regulations that were meant to keep us safe as we grow up and sometimes we single out a habit we saw them do on our own.

I remember one habit I picked up from my mother. Whenever I managed a project at work I would always try to get the project completed as soon as possible. I would press the staff to complete the project even if we had plenty of time to do it. One day I remembered back to when I was a little boy when my father would ask for something from me. My mother would get up from her seat and rush me through it prompting me and saying hurry, hurry your father asked you for something, hurry. No matter what he asked for the pressure to complete it was always on. Once I realized that, my mother placed this attitude in me, I was able to place it aside, and I became calmer and eventually I stopped driving the staff crazy.

There was also a time in my life that I would go to the racetrack every Saturday and I did this because it was the pastime of my brother-in-law's. I thought I liked it and I did it for fifteen years until one day, as I looked deeper into why I did it. I realized that this was not for me and from that moment on I never went to the racetrack again. I realized that I was at the racetrack only because I wanted to please someone else and be part of the group.

You must be like the fishermen and haul the net in which is your life and look at each thing about yourself and your habits and see if they are yours or do they belong to someone else. Then if you discover that they are not yours you can easily discard them. This is the process you must go through to find out who you are. When you begin this process you will gain a better understanding of the people in your life. This understanding of others will help you in your family, work and relationships. You will be able to help others find themselves as well. You will learn to unpack yourself and repack yourself without discarding anything and you will learn your true personality.

Acceptance of self

Accepting ourselves is one of the most difficult tasks we will have in life. Once we accept ourselves, life becomes so much easier.

There was a young convert who approached his pastor with a question. He said, "How can God forgive a sinner? Isn't God repulsed with all of the hatred and jealousy that fills the sinner's heart?" The pastor looked at the young man and said, "You are the third generation in a family of master furniture makers. Tell me this, if a fine table that your grandfather made was scratched would you throw it away?" "Of course not," the young man said. "A scratch doesn't alter the character of a fine piece of furniture." Then the pastor said, "If you nicked a well crafted oak rocker would you throw that away?" "Throw it away?" the young man said. "Even with a few scratches it's still quality furniture and is sturdy and valuable." The pastor said, "You have spoken like a true craftsman." "You share that same spirit with our creator who continues to find his human creation precious and valuable in spite of their obvious flaws."

As we go through life we get scratched and dented because of some of the choices we have made as we try to find ourselves. But these things have made us who we are and accepting them allows us to know our true character. We are all pieces of fine furniture in God's house.

Finding who you are will take the rest of your life. When I was studying to be a spiritual director one of the exercises we were given was to do something and then sit and see what we felt inside. When we would feel an emotion within ourselves we would ask the question, "Where is this from?" And in a short while the answer would surface. We would know if it was our parents, friends or just a circumstance in life that made this feeling surface. When we knew where it was from just the understanding of it would be enough to heal us and we would accept the feeling.

Each time you do something be open and ask the question, where is this from, is this mine or has someone else placed this in me. Then each day you awake you become a new person because of the decisions you have made in the previous day. Before, understanding these things and where they came from may have caused us to become down on ourselves. We may not have liked what we did because of the conflict between this impulse and our true selves. But all of the things we find should not be tossed away. They are to be accepted, understood and allowed to stay as part of you. Once you reorganize yourself you will see how all of these things have come together to form the character within you and nothing is wasted.

Acceptance of life

We must not only accept ourselves, we must accept our lives and what comes along each day.

There was a man who always bothered God with requests all day and night. One day God was tired of all the requests from this man and he said to him I will give you three wishes you can use for the next five years but during those five years you can't ask for anything else. The man was delighted and he thought for a moment and said to God I want to be rid of my wife she is always nagging me to do things around the house; she takes away my freedom. God said done. The man went home and he saw a large crowd around his home and as he approached he was told that his wife died. The man made arranged a funeral service and the whole town came and people spoke of how she was a good woman and how she helped them in their need. They said what will we do without her? The man began to see how good a person his wife was and how wrong he was to ask God to take her out of his life so he called on God. And he said to God, "I didn't realize how wonderful my wife was so I would like to use my second wish to get her back." God said done. The man went home and there was his wife as though nothing had happened.

Five years passed and each day the man would try to think of a wish that would make him happy, realizing that this was his last wish he didn't want to waste it. When the time passed for the man to make his final wish God appeared to the man and said, "I want to settle our account now make your last wish." The man said I don't know what to wish for." God said you must use it. So the man said to God "You tell me what I should wish for. God laughed and said I will tell you what to wish for, to be content with what comes along; then you will have true happiness in this life.

That's true happiness, to accept ourselves and what comes along in life. Not to try to change it to what we think it should be. For years I lived this way and it works just fine. I practiced this and I am always surprised and happy no matter what happens. It all becomes a great learning experience. Living this way let me experience true life and contentment.

Attitude towards life

Many years ago, a woman went to her doctor with a list of complaints about her health. The doctor examined her thoroughly and became convinced that there was nothing physically wrong with her. He suspected it was her negative outlook on life. It was her bitterness, fear and resentment that were the key to her feeling the way she did.

The wise doctor took the woman into a room in his office where he kept some of his medicine. He showed her a shelf filled with empty bottles and he said to her: "See those bottles? Notice that they are all empty. They are shaped differently, but basically they are all alike. Most importantly, they have nothing in them. Now, I can take one of these bottles and fill it with enough poison to kill a human being. Or I can fill it with enough medicine to bring down a fever, or ease a throbbing headache, or fight bacteria in one part of the body. The important thing is that I make the choice. I can fill it with whatever I choose."

The doctor looked her in the eye and said, "Each day that we are given is basically like one of these empty bottles. We can choose to fill it with love, life affirming thoughts, and attitudes, or we can fill it with fear that causes destructive and poisonous thoughts. The choice is ours."

One of the most important choices we make each day is the choice of attitude. It will either bring us happiness and harmony or negativity and discord. This choice is so important that whenever I held a sales training session I would begin by reminding them that when they came into the office I greeted them all differently. Some I would extend a hand, others a nod and others just a smile. In each case the person I was greeting would do the same. I would begin by saying "What you give is what you get." As you engage a person in conversation at work or family whatever your first move is they will do the same. If you are happy they will respond the same way. If cautious they will again respond the same. Attitude is a choice we make each day and you must remember what you give is what you get. Give anger and you will get anger, give gentleness and that is what you can expect in return. But the choice is ours.

When we look at life with a negative eye we lose sight of the beauty around us. In the mid 90's New York had a few ice storms and I can remember one night looking out of the front window of my home, there was a full moon that night and when I looked out the view took my breath away. I can remember thinking that never again would I be able to see such beauty. The ground shimmered from the reflection of the moon. I looked at the trees and could see how the ice formed on them making the tree look like it was made of fragile glass. Some trees had clear ice on them and others had a cloudy type of ice. The moonlight reflecting off these trees was so beautiful and seeing this made me feel peacefulness within myself. It was almost as though God had created this scene just to show us how beautiful and powerful God's touch could be.

The next morning I went to work and as usual was greeted by the guard who grumbled about how terrible the weather was, how cold and bitter and gray the sky was and how ugly it looked and how he wished it was summer again. I thought there was something wrong with me, and what I was seeing. When I got to my office I asked the young woman who sat in the next office to look outside and describe what she saw and to my surprise she said the same thing the guard said. She saw no beauty, only inconvenience.

Then I asked her to lift her eyes three feet off the ground and tell me what she saw and as she looked her expression changed and she said it looked like a picture post card and described the beauty of the trees covered with ice. When a person gets up in the morning they can choose to have a positive attitude and can see the beauty of the world around them or have a negative attitude and only see inconvenience and drudgery. Some people will say I hate Mondays or it's cloudy outside what a terrible day. Others say thank God it's Friday. All of these attitudes set the tone of their day. It's better to say how good the rain is as it washes and feeds the plants and how good it is to have some shade for a while. We are the women in the story who realized that each day is like an empty bottle and whatever attitude we put in our day is the way the day will go.

There is an exercise I give people who are caught in a negative attitude and that is to sit quiet and repeat the words, "How lucky I am, how grateful I am." And as you say this phrase, all good thoughts come to mind and your attitude will become positive.

Proper expectations

A few years ago there was a Governor running for re-election. The Governor had a grueling schedule. And one of the stops he had to make was at a Sunday afternoon barbecue. Politicians go to these functions so they can act like one of the common people.

On this particular day he was running late, and he was especially hungry. When he arrived at the barbecue he picked up a plate got on line, and put his dish out. At which time a woman on the other side of the table placed one piece of chicken on his dish.

He looked at the small piece of chicken and asked the lady for another piece of chicken "I have been running all day and I am very hungry." The woman said "I'm sorry, one piece of chicken to each person", but the governor said, "I'm starved", and again she said "only one to a customer".

The Governor decided to use the weight of his office to get another piece of chicken. So he said, "Madame, do you know who you are talking to?" I am the governor of this great state." And she answered, "Do you know who you are talking to? I'm the lady in charge of chicken. Now move along mister". The governor, because of his title, expected more, but he was disappointed.

Expectations are not goals, but are rules we place on ourselves, we also place them on the shoulders of others, if they wish to have a good relationship with us. There are proper expectations and unreasonable expectations. We should have proper expectations, which are needed to build a good foundation in which we can grow in our relationships and our self-esteem. Proper or reasonable expectations take time to form in us and strengthen our character. In a relationship we need to take into account what the person we are with is capable of giving. In ourselves we require the same consideration of time to see if what we are expecting of our abilities can be accomplished. When we set proper expectations our disappointments are few and far between.

When we create expectations that are beyond our abilities we set ourselves up to be disappointed. Unreasonable expectations are things we accept without giving thought if others or we can live up to them.

Expectations can be set in our minds as we watch a television program or an advertisement, people we come in contact with can place expectations in us and by our choices we make them our own. In creating unreasonable expectations, on others or ourselves, we lose our freedom.

An example, most of us can relate to, is the raising of a child. Parents form in their minds, what their child will be and how it should act before it is born. The parents may want the child to be a craftsman, a carpenter, a lawyer or whatever. The child on the other hand may like the arts and want to enter into a different field to support themselves. The child's heart is not in accord with what the parents have chosen for it and so the child begins to disappoint the parents.

The same child gets married, and the parents have an expectation of how they should be treated by this child and their spouse and how much they should be involved in the child's life after the marriage. Once again they are disappointed because they are not treated the way they expected.

We get a new job and agree to a salary and in the beginning we are content. Then one day we do a little extra work; newer people come into the company, during the time we work there we give the company and managers our honesty and loyalty. We feel that we should be treated better than the newer employee. We expect this because we have time in, we have paid our dues we are good corporate citizens. These are once again false expectations we create for ourselves that cause us to be disappointed.

Sometimes we don't allow enough time to enter into the depth of a situation to understand what our true expectation should be. We just move too quickly. In life it is better to take time and understand the nature of a person or project before we form our expectation, then we will not be disappointed. By allowing people a little freedom and time we will understand what they are capable of in a situation. Then by thinking things through at work we will understand that every payday we are even with the company; they owe us nothing and we owe them nothing. Realizing that every Monday we begin with a clean slate gives us a better perspective on life and a feeling of freedom. And don't expect a reward for loyalty and honesty because these qualities should be part of our character and should be part of all that we do.

Life unfolds for us each day and we see new things, situations and people that come into our lives. We don't always understand them or how they will fit in, so we uproot them as though they were weeds and toss them away. We didn't expect them to be or act the way we think they should. By forming expectations too quickly we may be tossing away great blessings that have been sent into our lives. But if you have patience and keep reasonable expectations of yourself and others you will not be disappointed and life's path will be smoother for you.

What causes the loss of our freedom?

One of the important gifts I have is freedom; the freedom to live and make choices, which are best for me and those around me. But the enemy of freedom is attachment. I found that so long as I was attached to something I could not be free. The attachments I speak about are the simple ones like habits, routines, and opinions of others.

As I looked back at my life I was surprised to find that I became attached to a routine, like doing the same thing on a Friday night. This left no room for new activities or adventures. It became a religion to me and held me prisoner. I found that if I didn't follow my routine I would get depressed or feel that the day wasn't going right. I would get attached to a certain way of interacting with people at work and when that would change I might get a little out of sorts.

I remember the day I realized that being attached to something takes away my freedom it was the day I bought a new car. After going to work and parking the car I went to my desk. During my first meeting I had trouble concentrating on the agenda because my thoughts were with the car. I thought to myself what if it gets scratched? Will someone park next to me and bang their door into my new car, or even worse would it be stolen?

I couldn't focus on my work; and I didn't give my full attention to the person I would be talking to. I wasn't working to my fullest potential any longer. That was when I decided that a car was not going to control my life. Once I decided that I regained my freedom and my life.

There is a story in the bible that explains how we get attached to things. There was a woodcutter in the forest who went about cutting trees down to build a home for himself. He made sure that he didn't waste one single piece of wood. When the house was finished he had one piece of wood that was about 5 inches long, but because he didn't want to waste it he sat down on the front porch of his home and he began to whittle a little figure out of it. When he completed the little figure he saw how beautiful it was. He thought that he should give it a place of honor in his new home. He decided he would put it on the window where the most light was coming into the house. Now each day he would pass it and he would admire the work he did and then one day he spoke to it.

Time passed and one morning when he was about to pass by this little object, he bowed to it. And from that day on each time he passed it he would bow until one day he knelt down and prayed to it. He would also ask this little figure for advice and over time this little useless piece of wood had become his God. He was unable to do anything without consulting this little figure. And that's how we begin to get attached to things.

We have our food in a certain way and that's the way we expect it. Soon, if we don't have it that way we think the day is ruined and the meal is ruined. We get up in the morning and we are used to having a sunny day and if it's raining we say what a terrible day this is going to be.

When we do this we begin to create a prison for ourselves in which we give up our freedom. We lose the freedom to make choices that we should make with ease.

The best way to overcome attachments is to do different things. Don't let your habit or routine take away your freedom.

How to regain freedom

Many years ago there was a man who was convicted of a small crime, which he didn't commit. The guards took him to the castle and put him in a dungeon. The dungeon was very dark except for a tiny window. Now each day the guard would open the door, place some bread and water on the floor and then close the door again.

This went on for about 20 years. This man lost his skills, his family, his work and all that was dear to him. One day he decided that he was going to take his own life. He could not go on any longer this way. He decided one evening, after the bread and water was put into the dungeon, he would proceed to hang himself. The night he was ready to do this he put the rope over the rafter, he got his chair in place and he waited for the guard to bring the bread and water.

That evening the guard came open the door and placed the bread and water on the floor. The man waited for the guard to go down the hallway and then he proceeded to check everything making sure that all was in order for what he was about to do. He tugged on the rope, made sure the chair was ready and then he went to the door to make sure that it was locked. He turned the handle of the door and to his surprise the door opened. He looked down the hallway to see if any guards were there and once again he was surprised that no one was there. He proceeded to walk down the hallway very slowly. He came to an open door and there the guards were playing cards. They looked at him very sternly, but they turned away and continued playing cards. He continued to walk slowly towards the front door where he met other guards, but they just looked at him as he made his way out the front door of the castle and he went home.

You see he was free all the time. All he had to do was to open the door and walk out. When we become attached to something we become a prisoner to that thing and we lose our freedom. We could become attached to a procedure, a person or an Idea that will hold us and can destroy us unless we let it go. As soon as we give up our attachments we regain our freedom and fear is destroyed.

You see he was free all the time. All he had to do was to open the door and walk out. When we become attached to something we become a prisoner to that thing and we lose our freedom. We could become attached to a procedure, a person or an Idea that will hold us and can destroy us unless we let it go. But as soon as we give up our attachments we become free. Free to make decisions and free of fear.

When you get a chance make a list of those things that you can live without and those you think you are attached to. Then begin to put them aside. Gently not violently, become unattached so that you could enjoy their pleasure and yet not be controlled by them.

Decide what's important to you

One day a professor was speaking to a group of his students and he wanted to drive home a point. He used an illustration that they never forgot. As he stood in front of the group of students he pulled out a one gallon, wide mouthed glass jar from under his desk and set it on the desk in front of them.

Then he opened one of the drawers of the desk and brought out some rocks about the size of his fist. He began carefully placing them in the jar one at a time. When the jar was filled to the top and no more rocks would fit inside, he asked, "Is this jar full?" Everyone in the class said, "Yes." Then he reached under the desk and pulled out a bucket of gravel. Then he dumped some gravel in and shook the jar causing pieces of gravel to work themselves down into the space between the big rocks. Then he asked the group once more, "Is the jar full?" By this time the class was on to him. "Probably not," one of them answered. "Good!" he replied. Again he reached under the table and brought out a bucket of sand. He started dumping the sand in the jar and it went into all of the spaces left between the rocks and the gravel. Once more he asked the question, is this jar full?" No!" the class shouted. Once again he said "Good!"

Then he grabbed a pitcher of water and began to pour it in until the jar was filled to the brim and nothing more could fit in the jar. Then he looked at the class and asked, what is the point I am trying to make here?" One eager student raised his hand and said, "The point is, no matter how full your schedule, if you try really hard you can always fit some more things into it! "No," the instructor replied, "that's not the point". The big rocks are the important things in your life and the, gravel, sand and water are the small every day things we do. The point is, if you don't put the big rocks in first, you'll never get them in at all.

Each day you have to decide what is important to you and then you must make sure that you set time aside to give your full attention to those things you have chosen. Things that are important can be family, friendship, work or personal growth. You may need time alone to unwind or reflect on the things of life that interest you.

Every morning that I get up I begin the day by making a list of things that I want to accomplish. The list can consist of making a phone call, researching information on a project, writing a report, or some small activity that needs to be done. Usually my list consists of maybe five items and I say to myself not all of these things have to be done today, but if I can accomplish one or two of them I will feel that I have been successful.

At the end of the day I look over the list and I begin the new list for the next day by listing the unfinished things of today on tomorrow's list. Reflecting on my list in the evening lets me know that I have done at least one or two of the things I set out to do this morning and I can have the feeling of accomplishment.

Making a list helps me keep on the path that will help me grow in the direction I have chosen by doing things that need to be done. I remember one day I thought to myself, if I only accomplish one item per day at the end of the year I will have done 365 things that needed to be done.

The list should not be made up of things that are too difficult to accomplish, they should be slices of things that are of a larger picture. For instance I wouldn't put down, if I were a programmer, write a new doctor billing system. What I might write down is, begin gathering information for the doctor billing system. The next day I might write; analyze the information I gathered thus far and the next day I have an item about interviewing one or two people about the system. These little slices of things to be done help us to have a sense of accomplishment, a sense of being able to chip away at the mountain of tasks that need to be done and knowing full well that by one little activity at a time we will achieve the completion of the larger task.

When I make my list I not only place items that pertain to work. The list is mixed with things of family and spiritual welfare. I may put that I need to speak with one of the children, so they may see more clearly in a part of life they are going through, or just to call them and to say how proud I am of them as parents. I may place on the list something that reminds me to call a retreat house to see what a good time would be to go on retreat and what the subject matter is on the different retreats that are available. The few things I put on a list each day are those things that are important to me. I put them in my day first because they will help me to be a better, father, husband, worker, manager or person in general. All of the things on my lists define what kind of person I am or want to become and that choice is mine, and I control that.

Honor, valor and decorum

My father told me that there were three things in life that you should never loose, your honor, valor and decorum. To have honor make your word your bond, have valor and be brave in doing what is right and have decorum in the way you carry yourself or present yourself in all that you do. He said further that if you lose these, your life is over. No one will trust you, people will avoid you and all will take advantage of you and you will live in a constant state of fear.

If you are a person of honor you will find in business and in personal life that people will want to associate with you. They know that when you give your word they can count on you to fulfill your end of the bargain whether it is easy or difficult to do. The honor you have accentuates your life. If you are a manager and you honor your commitments you will be looked on as a person who can lead and be depended on. If you are a parent your children and spouse will live in the comfort that you can be depended upon to not abandon them in tough times because you have given your word. When you give your word to someone you must live up to it

Valor goes hand in hand with honor. A person is called on in life to give their word to others and these people that you give your word to depend on you to be there, especially in the tough times. It's easy to give your word to someone and live up to it during the easy times but when the going gets a little tough we tend to give in and take the easy way out. Taking the easy way out during tough times can happen because you may be experiencing a loss of courage. It may come from selfishness or laziness or some other thing that causes you to lose courage and in turn not live up to your commitment. So give your word with courage and stand fast to your commitments and you will gain the respect of others.

The third of the trio is decorum. Decorum is the delivery system for honor and valor. Decorum comes from having character or style in the way you execute the commitments you have made. If you are a father, carry yourself as a man that sets good example for his children and his spouse. If you are a salesman represent your product or service properly. Look at the titles in your life and you will know how to carry yourself. Manager implies that you will plan your work in harmony with the rest of the management team. It means that you will look after the welfare of those working with you and help them to grow through the sharing of you knowledge. It means that when there are difficult times you will stand fast in truth and honesty doing what's best for all.

So guard these three with your life, because without them you have no life.

Distractions

Once you decide what's important to you always try your best to keep on target. There will be distractions, but it can be overcome by reminding yourself what your goal is.

Many years ago I had a dream about being on a journey to a mountain. Getting to the mountain was the goal for me and I could see the mountain very clearly. The beginning steps were very easy. As I got closer to the mountain there was a forest of very tall trees that surrounded the mountain. As I moved into the forest, I remember that I had to climb one of the trees each morning to see if I was still on the mark of moving toward the mountain.

One day as I moved closer to the mountain, I came upon a group of people that were relaxing in a clearing that had a stream nearby. They invited me to stay and rest with them and I did for a few days but when I wanted to continue towards the mountain they tried to talk me into staying with them. They were comfortable and they were enjoying life.

Although it was tempting I moved on because I remembered my goal that I wanted to achieve. Along the way there were other places I stopped to rest but I never abandoned my goal. As I got closer to the mountain I saw that there were other mountains that I could journey to; but I wouldn't have seen them had I not traveled to the first one.

I have found that I need a goal to aim each day. As a reminder I take notepaper and I write pieces of what I would like to achieve and what could be accomplished that day. As I do this I find that I am focused and have a general direction in which I need to travel. Some days I can't finish all that I have written down and some days I find new roads to take. The path to my goal may change a little but I always see my destination in sight.

As for the people I met along the way those are the ones who try to make me accept something less than the goal I could achieve. I always stop with them for a while but I continue on to reach my goal.

So never lose sight of your goal. Always take little steps each day to reach it. Your goal should not control you but should lead you to a path that will show you new possibilities and adventures.

Relationships - Interactions with others

Whether you are trying to build a relationship with one person or a group the rules are the same. You need to understand where the person or persons are coming from; you need to make decisions as to where the relationship is going. You need to hold it together with the glue of communication. You need to have a balance in the relationship and you must decide to either give life to the relationship or to take it away. So whether it's your work or an intimate relationship, you need to follow the rules.

Understanding people

I read somewhere many years ago that people never have difficulty interacting with nature. They love the trees; they love the grass; and they love the bushes. But they love these things because they don't talk back. It's very easy to get along with a tree you could say whatever you want it doesn't get hurt; it doesn't strike back at you; it just listens.

People on the other hand have a lot of emotions inside of them and they operate on different levels of consciousness. Each one has a different view of the world. Sometimes I marvel at the fact that we can even understand each other at all. When you enter into a relationship with another person, you both move into a sacred place, a place where you share intimate things. This place is entered whether you are selling something to a person or you are committing your love to each other. It is a place where we speak truth, we show respect for the person we are speaking with and we allow freedom of thought and emotion to rein between us.

Relationships can't be rushed, they grow slowly and they need patience and understanding. It is like two people dancing together for the first time. They move in the general direction as they should and in the beginning they may get out of step and step on each other's feet but eventually they get the rhythm and the dance goes smoothly.

To enter into a deep relationship with someone we must first understand that the person we are speaking to lives in a different world, a world they have created and are comfortable in. We must choose our words carefully as we realize that we are entering into their world and introducing some of our world to them. When we do this it must be done extremely gently making sure that you do not destroy or say anything derogatory about the world they've created for themselves. When the time comes that you want to leave the conversation you must gently close the door behind you so they remain in comfort. How you do this is up to you. Just realizing that they live in a different world will help you to be more gentle and considerate.

As you enter into the world of another person it's like going to someone's home for the first time. You greet them and tell them how much you appreciate being invited to their home. You compliment what you see and begin to speak about something you have in common. Then the conversation will move to a deeper level in which the home disappears and all that remains is you and the person growing your relationship through discovery and decision.

Discovery and decision – The foundation of relationships

Relationships grow by discovery and decision. Picture a young boy in his teens going into lunchroom, he looks across the lunchroom and he sees a pretty girl. He thinks to himself, that's a pretty girl. If I ever have the opportunity I would say hello to her. He has discovered the pretty girl and he made a decision.

The next time he sees her in the lunchroom and he is on line waiting to pay for his meal. He finds himself standing next to her and he looks at her tray and he sees carrots. He says; I see you like carrots I do too. She smiles and says yes.

They go their separate ways and the boy has discovered that he felt comfortable speaking to her and decides that the next time he sees her he will talk to her again. She on the other hand is making similar discoveries and decisions of her own.

A few days later he sees her having lunch by herself and he stops and asks her if he could join her for lunch, she says yes and they talk for quite a while. He feels good about the lunch encounter and decides to ask her out on a date soon. And so this process of discovery and decision continues until one day they marry.

Each relationship is based on discovery and decision some days we like what we discover and other days we may not. If we move gently into the relationship respecting the feelings of the other person we will have more successful encounters then we thought possible.

You might say that discovery and decision are the brick and mortar of any relationship. Discovery and decision will help you to raise your children. Each time you make a discovery in the things they choose to do, you will discover what adjustments need to be made to help them grow to be people of good character.

Discovery and decision helps in a relationship between two people because it shows them how to please each other so they can grow closer. Discovery and decision not only informs you of the things you like in a person to continue the relationship, but it also makes you alert to the times when you should be doing something to enhance the relationship.

Holding the relationship together – Communication

There was a young boy who spent a month every summer with his parents in an old farmhouse. Now the house was at least 150 years old when his family bought it. This house had never been modernized. The water supply during those years came from an old well that stood just outside the front door. This well was remarkable because it never ran dry. Even in the severest summer droughts, the old well faithfully had cool, clear water.

One day the boy's father decided to modernize the house. Part of the renovation was to drill a new well with an electric pump about a hundred feet from the house. He also decided to cap the old well and keep it as a reserve. The old well remained covered for several years until one day, moved by curiosity, the boy now a grown young man, decided to uncover and inspect the old well's condition. As he removed the cover, he fully expected to see the same cool, water he remembered so well as a boy. But to his surprise the well was bone dry.

It took him a while but the boy found out what had happened to the well. He learned that this type of well is fed by hundreds of tiny underground channels called rivulets, along which seeps a constant supply of water. As the water is drawn from the well, more water flows into it along these tiny channels, keeping them clear and open. But when a well like this is not used and the water is not regularly drawn, the tiny rivulets, or channels close up and the well becomes dry.

Just like the old well, when communication stops relationships end. Communication adds depth to any relationship, whether it is with a friend or it is with a group working on a project. It is communication that causes an exchange of ideas that lets us find a common level of being and purpose with others. It also allows us to strip away any masks or agendas we may have had and clearly shows our humanity and our honest intention for the other person or persons.

As we communicate and talk of our ideas the more we learn about ourselves and what we have in common with those around us and the goal we are trying to reach. But when communication stops friendships die and misunderstanding sets in and imagination takes the upper hand. Once that happens we become adrift and eventually lost.

Thoreau in his writings at Walden said that each day he made it a point to speak to someone in order to have balance. He said we need the human voice and conversation to keep our bearings. So each day he would travel into the town and find a person to have a short conversation with. It didn't matter who it was, it could have been the mailman on the road or a child but no matter what, he made it a point to speak with someone.

Communication brings life, depth, understanding, friendship and right thinking. In order to have life you need communication with your friends, fellow workers, family and God. When you lose communication with any of these you begin to descend into isolation and your relationships end and decisions become harder.

Finding the balance in a relationship - Triangles

There once was a wise and beloved king who cared greatly for his people and wanted only what was the best for them. The people knew the king took a personal interest in their affairs and that he tried to understand how his decisions affected their lives. From time to time, the king would disguise himself and wander through the streets, trying to see life from their perspective.

One day he disguised himself as a poor villager and went to visit the public baths. Many people were there enjoying the fellowship and relaxation. Now the water for the baths was heated by a furnace in the cellar, where one man was responsible for maintaining the comfort level of the water. The king made his way to the basement to visit with the man who worked so hard to keep the furnace going. The two men shared a meal together that day, and the king became a friend to this lonely man. Day after day, the king went to visit the fire tender, until one day the king revealed his true identity to his friend. The king's new friend looked into his eyes and said, "You left your comfortable palace to sit with me in this hot and dingy cellar. You ate my meager food and genuinely showed you cared about what happens to me. On other people you might bestow rich gifts, but to me you have given the greatest gift of all. You gave me the gift of yourself; you gave me your friendship."

The greatest gift we can receive from someone is their friendship or attention. But when we feel that we are not receiving our fair share we can get upset or depressed. This is because we feel that the person is not giving us the share of love, respect, openness, belonging or acceptance that we feel we deserve.

Several years ago, in the seminary, we had what was called a relationship weekend and in that weekend there was a segment called triangles. The presenter told us that all relationships form a triangle. Imagine at the first point of the triangle is you, the second your wife and the third your mother-in-law. As long as you are all equidistant, all is fine, but as you move one of the people closer to the other you will begin to alienate the third, making them feel as though they don't belong.

This may be why when a couple gets married and the woman spends too much time with her mother the husband will begin to be upset and feel that he is losing control of his family unit. This is the same for a woman when the husband spends too much time with his father or mother. As I listened to the presenter I began to imagine the makeup of the triangle differently. Suppose there were you, your wife at two of the points of the triangle and work was on the third. Now if you move too close to your work your relationship with your wife goes off balance.

For the next week I began to use the triangle concept with all of the things in my life like hobbies, projects, managers, people who worked for me, and I began to learn about some of the things in my life that made me feel alienated and of the people I may have alienated. This was a great reflection tool to know some of the things I needed to change and those things I needed to address in others who were in relationship with me.

Till today I use the triangle concept to make sure I am giving enough attention to the things and people in my life with proper balance.

We have the power to give life or take it away.

There is a story about a businessman who was hurrying down a busy street in Manhattan. This man was trying to make up time because he was late for an appointment. As he moved down the street he saw a poor man who was sitting on the side of a building selling flowers. The flowers were in an old cardboard lid and next to them was an old coffee cup with a few quarters in it.

The businessman dropped a dollar bill into the cup and continued on his way. But as he got about half way down the street, the businessman turned around and made his way back to the poor flower seller. "I'm sorry," the businessman said, to the man selling the flowers, "In my haste I failed to take my purchase. The businessman looked carefully at all of the flowers and then picked one out. After all, you are a businessman just like me he said. Your flowers are fairly priced and of good quality. I trust you won't be upset with my forgetting to pick out my purchase." With that he smiled and quickly went on his way again.

A few months later, the businessman was having lunch in an exclusive restaurant, when a neatly dressed handsome man approached the businessman's table and introduced himself. He said, "I'm sure you don't remember me, and I don't even know your name, but your face I will never forget. You are the man who inspired me to make something of myself. I was a vagrant selling flowers on a street corner until you gave me back my self-respect and a sense of dignity. You gave me hope and reminded me that I too was a businessman; you gave me my life back.

By our word or example we have the power to give life or take it away. We take away life when we become too critical of a person, especially someone close to us like a child or a spouse. What we say and do either makes for a good relationship or a destructive one. That choice is up to each of us.

In every situation we find ourselves in we should try to encourage others to be the best they can be. Encouragement is how we change the world to be a better place. Encouragement of others brings about growth within a person. When two people get married they need the encouragement of their families and friends in order to grow in the new life they have chosen. Always do the best you can to build confidence in others through encouragement, and remember to treat them with great dignity so they remember who they should be.

Stages of life – Collecting, trading and releasing

One day I was monitoring a telemarketing call. The telemarketer was trying to sell an appointment with a prospect. As I listened I heard a man who was totally relaxed and didn't want anything to do with our services. He was extremely polite and kind to the young lady who was making the call. After some time the prospect wanted to end the call and he said, "I don't need anything that you are selling because I am retiring and I am looking to sell my business." At that the telemarketer said goodbye and hung up. I called the telemarketer and said to her to call back and ask him if he wanted us to sell his business for him and we would handle the transaction. She called him back and proposed what I said and she got the appointment.

What I learned from this call was that there are three stages in life; collecting, trading and releasing. This man on the phone was in the releasing stage of his life. In life we all pass through these stages. When we are young we collect worldly things and friendships and we hold on to them tightly. Then we come to a point that we would rather make better use of the things we have and we begin to trade. We trade one job for another, one career for another, this friend for that one, and this house for a larger one. But in the final stage we look for simplicity. We want to rid ourselves of the things that weigh us down or that we don't need. We sell our home for a smaller one, we release some friends because too many confuse us and we look for that peaceful existence we feel that we deserve. This is where the man on the phone was at the time of our call to him; he was looking for a simpler life, a time to reflect and enjoy the rest of his life.

As I learned about the sales process I learned more about people and the way they react in and to life. Life in itself is a sales process. We are always trying to sell the only product we know, which is our view of life or a situation or ourselves. We sell ourselves to our family and friends. We sell ourselves to God. We sell ourselves to all the people we meet and we try to show them how good we are or how much we know or can do.

When we speak to someone we need to know which stage of life they are in, so we can find that one common ground that lets us talk and find comfort in our conversation. It takes time to enter into depth and find out what stage someone is in, but it's worth it.

Competition can destroy

For the past 18 years I've managed a direct marketing group for J.P. Morgan Chase. In that time one of the greatest lessons I learned was not to let the employees compete with each other. In the group there was a technical staff, a person who worked on strategies, a telemarketing group and a group that did the mailing of promotional items or letters.

I first learned the lesson about competition as I was training the telemarketing group. All of the telemarketers came from companies that forced them to compete. Because competition fosters the attitude to win or be the best at all cost, they tended to forget about quality. The contests consisted of who would get the most appointments or who was able to sign up the most new customers. When we compete we are tempted to sell something the customer doesn't need just to win. With this approach you will find that some of the prospects just say yes to get you off the phone.

When we started out I allowed the competition within the group. But as time went on I noticed that when you have a winner you have to have a loser. The winner began to be filled with self-pride and the losers became depressed and I would have to spend part of my day lifting their spirits.

In the group, I had one telemarketer that would bring in 15 to 20 appointments a day. I also had another telemarketer who would bring in five or six each day. The person who brought in five or six appointments always felt depressed and he began to feel that he didn't belong in the group. But what I found was that the telemarketer who brought in five or six appointments came up with more quality appointments then the one who brought in 15 to 20.

So one day I decided to try something different. I told the telemarketers that we would not allow competition in the department. What they needed to do was to compete against themselves so the person who is doing 20 appointments should look at the quality and if the quality was only five or six good appointments he should compete against himself and try to make that seven good appointments or at least break even for the day. The one who can only bring in five appointments they would compete against themselves by trying to bring in six one day and again if they broke even that was okay.

This began to work very well and I found that there were no losers in the group. Everyone's performance began to increase and their attitude was better towards each other. I know it's unusual to run a group by reprimanding somebody who competes but I found that competing can cause separation in the group. This was more destructive to the group than anything else.

This worked well in this group so I extended it to the other groups. Whenever a project was completed the user group would send us either a basket of fruit or pay to have the one or two individuals responsible for the project to be taken out to lunch.

The way I changed this was that each time a user wanted to take a few people to lunch we would request that a less expensive lunch or cookies and coffee be brought in for all to enjoy. Those who gave up the lunch so the others could share in the good fortune liked it even more because the employees who received the benefit for the work they did, thanked them and congratulated them for a job well done. It made the other groups want to share when they had something good offered to them for a job well done.

I began to find that the groups were rooting for each other to deliver a good quality job because when one of the groups succeeded everyone would benefit from the reward. We went so far as one of the projects was done well the group and that was acknowledged and received a full day off with pay. All the other groups who worked with them, but had nothing to do with that project, would receive the benefit of half a day off.

I also found that sometimes time off was far better for the employee and then a small amount of money or a lunch. They used this found time like taking a Friday afternoon off or a Friday off to do all the chores you have to do on Saturday. This way they could enjoy the whole weekend with their families. What I learned from this management style was that when you treat people like human beings they respond with loyalty and good quality work. Corporations were created to support families; families were not created to support corporations. You should love people and use things, not love things and use people.

Over the years we had the lowest turnover rate of any department in the company. I had a mixture of temps and full time employees. If you were a temp you became a candidate for the next job opening in the department. We started with three employees and grew to 30, with 20 temps in addition.

Some of the temps stayed with us for 12 years. That is because we treated them like family.

We never treated a temp different than an employee of the bank even when we received a bonus. They weren't on the payroll yet we would all put some money into a pool for them to share or we would take them out to lunch to show our appreciation for the work they've done.

All of these wonderful things came out of the fact that I learned that competition belongs on the baseball field or in sports, but it does not belong in the workplace. It tends to cheapen the work and cause dissension and depression within the employees and the groups.

The same rules apply to family. Each person in a family should never be compared to the attitude or the skills of another family member or person. They should be judged based on what they bring to the table. If one member is successful, all should share in that success in some small way. Do this and you'll find not only will you have a happy staff and you will also have a happy family and a good life. Just remember competition can destroy a person, family, marriage friendship, group or company.

When you have a winner they stand on the shoulders of the loser. If you never win in a competition your self-esteem will begin to be destroyed. If you compete with each other in a marriage, you will find that you are living with a person that you love but you don't like them and that makes for an unhappy marriage.

The most important relationship

The most important relationship you will have in your life is with God. Without a solid relationship with God, all other relationships and activities will seem less fulfilling. This relationship with an unseen being is difficult to grow because it takes faith to deal with the unseen and all we have are a few notes to guide us; like the spiritual writings our ancestors left us. Although we can't see, touch or feel God we can see reflections or shadows of his presence through what we do and through our relationships with others.

Take a moment and imagine if you had to explain the color red to a person born blind from birth. The person would look to their faculties to try to understand what you're describing. Because they can't see, and never have, what they might say is the color red hot or cold. They will ask us whether it's hard or soft. Based on these questions we would never be able to explain the color red to them. And so it is with God we don't have the faculties to see him as he is. We just see a shadow or his interaction in our lives with others after the fact.

We can only see God based on where we have been in life. Picture a boat on the ocean. You could only tell it's been there after it has passed when you see its wake. As it is with us, we can only see God after he has been there and we do this through reflection.

To help your relationship grow you need to take time at the end of your day and reflect to see where God has been with you today. Cherish this relationship and help it to grow within your heart so that you understand God's motion within you. One day when you truly are called home to be with him you will say hello old friend, rather than who are you?

Living your faith

In this section I have placed some of the tools needed to get a person through the difficult parts of life. When we come to a difficult part of life we sometimes lose sight of what's important or the direction we should be going in.

Some of the challenges we face in life are great and others are small personal challenges we must overcome, but in all of these challenges we must keep in mind that how we proceed must not be ego driven. They must be driven by right thinking and for the greater good of you, your family and the community. If the challenge before you is ego driven, you will cause damage to yourself and your relationships. The outcome could be destructive to you character and honor.

Before entering into a challenge you must think deeply and if you discover that it is selfish, then walk away from it. But remember the walking away from an ego driven challenge will be the true challenge for you.

Perseverance

Mount Everest is 29,000 feet high. In 1952 Edmund Hillary attempted to climb Mount Everest. Edmond Hillary failed. A few weeks later a group in England asked him to address its members. Mr. Hillary walked onto the stage to the sound of thunderous applause. The audience was recognizing his attempt at greatness, but Edmund Hillary saw himself as a failure. He moved away from the microphone and moved to the edge of the platform. He made a fist and pointed at a huge picture of Mount Everest. Then he said in a loud voice, "Mount Everest, you beat me the first time, but I'll beat you the next time, because you have grown all you are going to grow... but I'm still growing".

On May 29, 1953 Edmond Hillary climbed Mount Everest, to the very top. For his accomplishment he was knighted and became Sir Edmond Hillary. Sir Hillary didn't know it at the time but he had to grow into this success to conquer the mountain he faced. To do this he had to keep trying, he had to have perseverance.

We all have a Mount Everest that we **must** climb and like Sir Edmond Hillary we may not succeed the first time we **try**. For each person the Mount Everest we must climb is different. Some **of the** challenges we face may look easy to the person next to us, but to us **they** are a real challenge.

Some years ago I had surgery and the recovery process was my Mount Everest. Each day I got up and had to struggle to take a medication that didn't agree with me. The medication would give me stomach pains and it took away the little energy I had. But each morning I got up I tried to walk and move a little further then I did the day before. Some mornings I couldn't match what I did the day before, but through perseverance I became stronger then the illness and I regained my strength back.

There were many Mount Everest's that challenged me in my life. I had the Mount Everest of becoming a manager, the Mount Everest of public speaking and in each challenge that appeared I would persevere taking one step at a time. With each step I would focus more and enter into depth challenging what had to be overcome.

Each person has a different Mount Everest. To some it is the challenge to find God in their lives, for others it could be overcoming writers block, and others just having to say you are sorry. But whatever it is the challenge must be faced.

Mount Everest appears in our lives every day and every day we make the climb. Many times we try but we end up failing, like Sir Edmond Hillary. But we must have perseverance like he did. We must remember Sir Edmond Hillary's words. "Mount Everest, you beat me the first time, but I'll beat you the next time, because you have grown all you are going to grow... but I'm still growing". If we try, God will always give us the knowledge and strength to grow greater than the challenge we have before us.

Serving others

There's a French fable that tells of how one day the Kings trusted personal servant went walking in a dense part of the forest near the palace. There he stumbled while stepping over a log and fell down a hill. As he was brushing off the leaves he looked down and saw a lamp. He went to clean it off by brushing it and there before his eyes appeared a genie.

The genie said finding this lamp was no accident, you've worked hard all your life. Now you may receive one wish. But be careful because you can have only one wish. The servant replied, all my life I have been in positions where I had to serve others. In fact I am known as the servant of the kingdom. In the future I want people to wait on me, and I want servants to do everything for me. Sure enough, when the man returned to the castle, the door was opened for him. His food was cooked, meals served, dishes washed and clothes cared for by others. He was not allowed to perform his usual work --- everything was done for him.

For the first month the newness of the experience amused him. The second month it became irritating. During the third month it became unbearable. So the man returned to the forest and searched the forest until he found the lamp. He rubbed it and the genie appeared again. The man said "I've discovered that having people wait on me isn't as pleasant as I thought it would be. I'd like to return to my original station in life and be the servant of the kingdom." The genie replied "I'm sorry I can't help you. I had the power to grant you only one wish". The man said "but you don't understand. I want to serve other people. I have found it more rewarding to do things for others than to have them do things for me." The genie just shook his head. The man said "please help me I'd rather be in hell then unable to serve others." The genie said sorrowfully, "Oh and where do you think you have been the last ninety days?" To be king you must serve and to serve you must give of yourself.

True happiness, wisdom and healing are found in serving others. Over the years I have found that the best way to learn something is to teach someone else what you have learned. Recently I was helping someone to learn how to use the computer and after he learned some of the basic instructions I ask him if he would kindly teach me what he learned. As he taught me he began to understand what he had just learned at a deeper level.

I have also noticed that in serving others we become healed. In our church was a woman who lost her husband and a child. The pain within her was very severe and to alleviate the pain she volunteered to go to one of our of consolation sessions in which people who suffered a loss in their family would share what they were going through. During the session as she began to tell her story she began to notice some of the heaviness began to leave her heart. There were others there who had felt the same way. At the end of the evening she felt much better. After that evening she became a regular and the more she came back to the sessions to find help for herself the more she noticed that she was helping others in the group to deal with their grief and slowly she began to heal. Her strength returned and she was able to live her life, as her husband and child would have wanted her to. So remember, to serve is to grow in strength, wisdom, and happiness.

When you're lost

From time to time we tend to get lost and we lose track of what we are doing or what we are about. It is in that time that we need to find a way to refocus our selves so we can begin again. But before you can find your way back on your path you must first admit you're lost.

There is an old story of a man who was lost in the forest. As he walked along his path he would see people and ask for directions; but they were also lost. Then after wandering in the forest for several hours he saw a castle in the distance and he began to run to it. He hoped he would get some food, rest for a while and get directions. As he approached the castle he saw other people near the castle but they didn't seem to notice it, they just walked by. He made his way to the door and knocked. After a few moments a man came and opened the door and he asked if he could come in for some rest, refreshments and directions. He said he had been traveling all day and was lost. The old man said come in, but the man hesitated. He said to the old man that he recognized some of the people who were passing by and he knew that they were lost too because they had asked him for directions. He wondered why they did not knock on his door. The old man said this is a magic castle and in order to see it and receive help you first must admit you are lost.

So the first step is to admit you are lost. Try not to hide the fact or you will just look foolish to everyone. The second thing you must do when you are lost is to go back to basics and begin the journey again.

Whenever we start a new project at work we come together and discuss what we are trying to accomplish. Most of the time people in meetings work for other groups and each one will try to gain control of the project. It's like having too many chiefs and no Indians. We had a meeting like that the other day and as usual we started to define what we wanted to do. But somewhere along the line we became confused and soon lost sight of the objective. Then a young woman named Maxine reminded us of something very basic that we should have all remembered. She said if we just follow the process it will bring us to the basics and that will get us back on track. Then the objective will become clear and we will find our way.

She was right. When we give ourselves up to a process the first thing that happens is that we become like children listening to our parents. And as we begin doing the basics one new door opens after another until we reach our destination.

Picture, if you can two people in a family who have had a disagreement. They are angry and filled with self pride over what they feel is an injustice done to them. If they continue this way they will destroy their family ties. But if they follow the process in the Gospel, not to judge but to forgive, then the next time they see each other, if they both say a simple hello, then the healing can begin. From that point on if they continue in simple conversation they will begin to grow beyond the anger and resentment in their hearts. The confusion will disappear and then they will begin to be family again.

One of the best examples of following the process is what happened on September 11th. . The next day people stopped what they were doing and went back to basics. They became like little children, people of all faiths began praying together. People of all walks of life stood together and began helping and consoling one another. They were following the healing process and in doing that they rebuilt their lives and their country.

The Gospel gets its power from actions, not words. It is a process to be lived each day at home and in business. And when we do this we give the Gospel meaning, by making the word of God a living reality in our own time and place. Take some time today and find something that is getting you down or has you confused and follow the process Jesus gave you. Within a short time your burden will be light and peace will follow.

Overcoming fear

Years ago, out west, a new prison was completed with much of the labor done by the prisoners themselves. The new modern structure was to replace the old prison that housed many prisoners for over a hundred years. After the prisoners were moved to their new quarters, they spent long tiring days stripping the old prison of lumber, electrical fixtures and plumbing that could be reused. Now all this was all done under the supervi¬sion of the prison guards.

As they began dismantling the jail walls, the prisoners were shocked and angry because they found out that, although huge locks were attached to the heavy doors and two inch steel bars covered the windows, the walls were made out of paper and clay painted to resemble stone and iron. It was obvious to all the prisoners that during their stay in the old prison, a hard kick would easily have knocked out the walls, allowing them to escape. But for many years these men were huddled in their locked cells, thinking escape was impossible. No one had ever tried to escape because it seemed that freedom was beyond their reach.

As we live our lives we create paper walled prisons for ourselves. We allow our thoughts, opinions and expectations of others to hold us prisoner. We also create prisons for ourselves by creating false responsibilities to carry out.

Some years ago I met a man who always made a task out of everything he did. Everything had to be perfect, and he had to have closure in everything. He was not patient when something needed to be done. He wanted it done right away. He not only wanted perfection from himself but he wanted perfection from the people in his office and in his family as well. He said, "As time passed he felt a bitterness growing within him." He didn't like his job because he felt that the people didn't know how to work as he did. He was upset with his family because they didn't see things his way on how they should live. He became bitter because no one could live up to his expectations. They were imperfect people doing inferior work as far as he was concerned.

Then one day he had enough. He stopped in church and he prayed to God. He said his life was too complicated and he didn't want to be responsible for others. He just wanted to do his own work and live his own life and let others work things out for themselves. He didn't want to correct people any more or fix their mistakes. He said to God, "You take care of them it's too much for me." He said, "It was the best decision he ever made and the results surprised him." As time passed he noticed that by leaving people alone they were able to work out their own problems. They would come up with solutions that he never considered before. He began to learn from them. He understood that by allowing people make their own decisions and mistakes it made them stronger and it gave him patience. At home he learned that there were other ways of living besides his own. He saw that when he gave things up to God and just paid attention to what he was responsible for he became peaceful and free. The walls of his prison came down.

Jesus said in the gospel today, "Come to me you who labor and are overburdened and I will give you rest." When we come to Jesus He first removes those false responsibilities and expectations that we have created for ourselves that weigh us down. It is when these things are removed that we have rest. So today place yourself before Jesus and with His help examine all of the things in your life that are too difficult for you to carry. Ask yourself if there are expectations you have of others, yourself, or God that cannot be fulfilled because they may be a little unreasonable, or too rigid? Are there routines that you have created that have become too heavy for you to carry? Then place these things at the feet of Jesus and remind yourself that you are not responsible for everyone or everything in the world, you just are responsible for the few things God gave you to do. When you do this you will have the freedom that you once had as a child. You will have broken the walls of your prison and you will truly be free and at rest.

Finding the path through trust and patience

Once there was a stream that was working itself cross country, and it had very little difficulty because it would run around anything that got in its way, like forests, rocks and mountains. Then one day it came to a desert. Just as it had crossed every other barrier, the stream tried to cross this one, but it found that as fast as it ran into the sand the waters disappeared. After many, many attempts it became very discouraged. It appeared that there was no way that the stream was going to cross the desert and continue its journey.

Then a voice came in the wind. It said to the stream," if you stay the way you are, you cannot cross the sands and you will be nothing more than a damp spot on the sand. To go further you must change, you will have to lose yourself." The stream said, "But if I lose myself I won't remember what I am supposed to be." "Quite the contrary," said the voice "if you have faith and lose yourself you will become more powerful than you ever dreamed you could be." So the stream listened to the voice in the wind and surrendered itself in faith to the sun, and it began to change into clouds and the wind carried the clouds to the other side of the desert. Then the sky thundered and lightening came and the clouds became rain and the little stream became a powerful river and continued its journey.

The decision to trust and have patience is within each person, but most of us would rather push our way through projects and tasks we face just like the little stream. But just like the stream found out there is a better way and the way is to trust in the paper and the information you have with patience. The project will reveal what needs to be done.

Several years ago I was given a project in which I was given a few notes and some general information about what had to be done. I remember thinking how will I ever sort this out? I began to look at the notes and began to separate them into groups. Some notes referred to timeframes of the project, other notes were the details of some of the segments to be done. There were notes on the goals of the project.

The first few hours I looked at the notes and just sat with what I had read not making any decisions or forming any opinions, just listening to the notes and where they were leading. Soon the notes began to reveal an order as to what had to be done. I began to separate the notes into categories of goals, timing, and details. As I did this I began to see that some segments were missing from the project, I began to make notes so they could be included. Also in the details I noticed that there were different levels.

I placed aside all of the time constraints and costs. By removing them, the project had a freedom to it and it began to show me the true sequence of events that should take place and who should be involved. Once the plan was in place I reapplied timing and cost. The project was successful and was more inclusive then the scattered approach I used to take in the past.

As each moment in life presents itself to you, if you take your time, it will be revealed to you what needs to be done.

Finding happiness

One day a boy and his parents were working in the fields when a severe storm came up suddenly. During the storm the lightning struck the boy's parents and they died instantly. The boy had no family and he didn't want to be put in a home, so he decided to go it alone. He never talked much but he worked very hard.

Time passed and he saved enough money to open a small repair shop where he fixed small farm equipment for the town's people. One day he met a woman. She was not what you would call beautiful but he fell deeply in love with her. There was nothing he wouldn't do for her. Once a month on the fourth Saturday he would take some of the money he had earned and he would take his wife into town and buy her something. One month he would buy her a dress and another time he would get her a hat but he always bought her something. He did this for several years until one day she died.

Sometime later he adopted a baby boy and he began the same thing all over again. Once a month on the fourth Saturday he would take his son into town and buy him something. At first it was a rattle then as he got older he would buy him a tie or a suit and so on. Now whenever he went into town the town's people would notice a sparkle in his eye.

One day one of the town's people went to see him in his shop. He was covered with grease. As I said he was a very quiet person, a man of few words. The visitor began to speak to him and said I am sorry for the bad luck you had in your life. I don't know how you deal with it. Now the farmer responded with that sparkle in his eye. He said, being happy is nothing more than having something to look forward to and helping those you love to have something to look forward to, and that's what gets us through the day.

I remember the time when I bought my first car. I came home one day from work and my father told me about a car one of the neighbors had for sale. It wasn't in the best condition; the windows didn't roll down, it needed tires and a few other things. But the person selling the car said they would wait a week or two until I could make arrangements to get the money. During those two weeks I can't tell you how happy I felt inside. I must have driven the car hundreds of miles and fixed so many things on the car in my mind before I got the keys. Looking forward to driving the car was better than driving it for me.

For each person what you have to look forward to is different. For some it's the morning when you get up and prepare yourself. For others it's the afternoon when you look forward to that time when the afternoon snack is coming. We all experience it. It's the excitement in the heart. My wife thinks I'm crazy and tells me how can you get excited over these small things and I tell her it's these small things I look forward to that make me happy.

Quick judgment

One afternoon a shopper at a local mall felt the need for a coffee break. She bought a little bag of cookies, put them in her pocketbook, and got in the line for coffee. She found a place at a table, took out a magazine to read, and sipped her coffee. Across the table sat a man who was reading a newspaper. She reached out and took a cookie from the bag on the table. As she did, the man seated across the table reached out and took one too. This put her off, but she did not say anything. A few moments later she took another cookie. Once again the man did too. Now she was getting a bit upset, especially since only one cookie was left now. Apparently the man also realized that only one cookie was left. He took it, broke it in half, offered half to her, and proceeded to eat the other half himself. Then he smiled at her, got up from his seat, put his paper under his arm, and walked off. Was she steamed! As she went into the parking lot to go to her car she opened her bag and reached in for the keys and to her surprise there were the bag of cookies she had bought! All the time she thought she was eating her cookies but they belonged to the man at the table. How embarrassing.

In this story the man is God. We are the woman. The bag of cookies belongs to God. The cookies are all of the things we have in our lives like homes, cars, family, children our friends and our talents.

Wouldn't it be nice if people in the office would read this story before a meeting? I think it would remind them that the meeting is not just for them but that the outcome has to be for the good of all involved as well as the company. So many times people go to these meetings and they are not open to the opinions and feelings of others. They look out only for their interest. God has given us a job which allows us opportunities to use our talents, support our families and build stronger communities. I also thought it would be nice if people would read this story at home. I think that they might realize that they do not own their families. Mothers and fathers are there to do their part as a member of the family. To place themselves second for their children so the children can learn by good example for their journey ahead.

Sometimes as a father I feel that my children are like my possessions to me, but then I come to my senses and realize that they are equal to me just a different age and with different jobs to perform, like learning how to share with others. And children would be reminded that all of life is a gift from God and their parents, brothers and sisters are their first gift. Through their family they will learn good morals, order and the value of relationships. So as they move into the world they will have respect for others. What God gives us as family is each other. If we remember the story before we meet with our friends we would act differently toward them knowing that they are not to be owned and molded by us but they are there to be loved just the way they are and they are there to love us as we are. God gives us friends, they are there to walk with us in life and to love us and be loved by us.

Jesus tells us today in the Gospel that we are renters here. We own nothing. All belongs to our gracious landlord. The only rent he wants us to pay is to be grateful and share the things we do and have with others. When we think we own the things we have in our lives we deny God's presence or existence. Sit today and list all of the things you have or have had in your life Say thank you to God that's all the payment He needs.

Doubt

There is a legend that tells about the time the devil decided to close his shop in one part of town and open in another. He got up early one morning and made a "going out of business sign" and placed it in the window. Now one of the customers was fascinated with the various instruments on display, but there was one in particular he noticed that had a high price tag. It was called doubt. The man asked the devil. "Why is this one so expensive?" "Quite simple." said the devil. "It's my favorite tool. With the tool of doubt I can pry into most everyone's life and cause all kinds of damage.

I know a woman who when she has dinner guests she says to the guests "This dinner didn't turn out right, it's awful." She doesn't realize it but she has just picked up the devils tool and doubted her abilities as a cook. Now she has laid the ground work for her to fail at other things. And soon she will think less and less of her abilities. There are other ways to pick up the devils tool of doubt and use it on ourselves. We get a bad review at work. Business slacks off. A cold hello, a bad report card, a broken promise, a bad relationship or I gained a few pounds. When these things happen to us we have the tendency to feel discouraged and then we lose confidence in our abilities and we give up.

The devil hands the tool off to people through gossip. When we speak badly of someone to another person, the person we are speaking to loses trust in the other person's ability. Doubt causes trust to be broken and when trust is broken it cannot easily be repaired. In the Gospel today Jesus meets a woman at the well who has made a mess of her life. She thought she could find happiness in the pleasures of this world. She thought eating, drinking and being merry would give her this wonderful happiness she was searching for, but it couldn't. She made vows to people and quickly broke them. Her fibs became lies. Loving and being loved became using and being used. The more this woman failed the more discouraged she became. Then Jesus says the words, "Give me a drink." In the confrontation that followed she found God loved her in spite of all she had done and that He was ready to help her find the living water within her so she could once again feel good about herself.

We are the woman at the well and in this Lenten season Jesus has come to meet us and heal us by letting us know he still loves us. He wants us to know, that it doesn't matter what we were. It doesn't matter what we are. The only thing that matters to Him is what we want to be. The devil follows us during this Lenten season, saying to us you failed, you broke your fast, it's not perfect, give it up. Our response should be no. We should do as Jesus did when He fell three times carrying the cross, we must get up and continue. If you do that you defeat the devil and his most precious tool becomes useless.

Lent is a time in which God shows us that all things are possible with love; His love for us. Take a few minutes today and close your eyes and picture yourself at the well and allow Jesus to show you how much He loves you and wants to heal you. Perhaps you will feel the life giving water within your heart flow once again.

Never quit

Ignacy Jan Paderewski, as a young boy was discouraged by his teachers from becoming a pianist and following the song in his heart. Thank God he decided not to listen to them and quit, because he became the most popular and famous pianist that lived in the last 100 years and earned the title "The master." In his list of accomplishments was the ability to speak seven languages fluently, he wrote two operas, a symphony, two piano orchestral pieces, a violin and piano sonata, several beautiful songs. He gave over 1500 concerts in the United States of which he gave the proceeds to feed the poor and help the unfortunate. They say each recital was a spiritual happening because he could make the piano sing. It was as though God placed his hands around him and made his music perfect.

Paderewski, the master, one night was scheduled to perform at one of the great concert halls in the United States. Present in the audience that evening was a mother with her fidgety nine year old son, who against his wishes had agreed to attend the concert. The young boy was tired of waiting, and he squirmed constantly in his seat. His mother had hoped her son would be encouraged to practice the piano, if he could just hear the immortal Paderewski at the keyboard. As she turned to talk with friends, her son could stay seated no longer. He slipped away from her side, and became drawn to the beautiful concert grand piano on the huge stage filled with bright lights. Without much notice from the sophisticated audience, the boy sat down at the stool, staring wide eyed at the black and white keys. He placed his small, trembling fingers in the right location and began to play "Chopsticks." The roar of the crowd was hushed as hundreds of frowning faces turned in his direction. Irritated and embarrassed, the audience began to shout: "Get that boy away from there." "Who'd bring a kid that young in here?" "Where's his mother?" "Somebody stop him!" Backstage, the master overheard the sounds out front and quickly figured out what was happening. Paderewski jumped up and grabbed his coat and rushed toward the stage. Without one word of announcement, he stepped over behind the boy, reached around him, and began to improvise a countermelody to harmonize and enhance "Chopsticks." As the two of them played together, Paderewski kept whispering in the boy's ear: "Keep going. Don't quit, son. Keep on playing.... Don't stop.... Don't quit now."

In this story we are the boy and the master is Jesus. When we come into this life we have a song in our hearts. As soon as we are old enough, we approach the piano of life we begin playing that little song we were born with.

Some have the song of the carpenter in their hearts others the office worker, there is the song of the doctor, the nurse, the teacher, the police officer. Some play the song of a parent and others the song of an aunt or uncle or a friend. No matter what the song we have been given, when we are ready, and we begin to play. The master hears us, and he comes onto the stage in our lives, and places his hands gently around us and plays a countermelody to harmonize and enhance "our song." And then, in that moment, all things are right. No song is ever off key if we allow the master to be with us. This is the season of Hanukah and Christmas and the master reminds us that he is there with us and ready to help us. And if we listen carefully today we can hear Him whispering in our ear, "keep playing, don't stop, don't quit, don't give up on yourself because I haven't and I never will.

We are God's skin

One night a little girl prepared herself for bed, when she was ready her parents tucked her in for the night. Around midnight the little girl woke up to the loud sound of thunder. She was frightened and began to cry. Her father rushed into her room to comfort her. The girl said to her father "I'm afraid please can you stay with me for a while and hold me?" Her father said "There is nothing to be afraid of we are right next door and we are here to protect you." Remember Jesus is here with you too. The father said goodnight to the little girl and he went back to his room. Within a few minutes the thunder got louder and the lightning flashed in her room and lit up the walls. The little girl began to cry again and her father once more rushed into the room to comfort her. Her father said once again, "Don't worry we are right next door and Jesus is with you. Nothing is going to happen to you." Remember how you learned in school that Jesus is always here and watches over you no matter where you are or what time it is. You may not see him but he is here protecting you. As her father moved toward the door the girl said please stay with me and hold me I'm still afraid. I know Jesus is here with me but right now I need somebody I can hold.

Jesus tells us today, that he is our shepherd, but we can't see him as we see other people. We can't feel his touch. We can't hear his voice. So how can he shepherd us? How will he guide us through the tough times in life?

I began to think about this and I remembered back to when I was in first grade. Each day about 10 in the morning several of the brothers would come into our classroom dressed in their dark brown albs' to visit us. As they came in, the room would brighten up as though someone special was with us and there was nothing to worry about. Their strong presence made us feel happy and we realized Jesus was present to us through them.

As the brothers made Jesus present to us in school, so too does a priest when he comes to the altar. We leave our world behind for a piece of time, the music starts, and we sing we stand together as one people. We have the feeling that we belong. We feel our connection to the congregation. We know that we are part of something greater then ourselves, we feel encouraged, and that we are of value to the world and that we make a difference. Jesus comes to us through others, to speak to us, to hold and comfort us, to love us to remind us that we are important, and to give order to our lives.

So remember that when you feel lost or lonely, God will make an appearance through someone you least expect. When you feel down it might just be the stranger who passes you on the street and smiles or nods that makes you feel that you have not been forgotten.

Hearing vs. listening

There was a woman who believed she had a hearing problem because she always had to ask her friends to repeat what had been said in a conversation. The woman one day made an appointment with a specialist to have her hearing checked. The doctor told her that he had the latest equipment, but that he preferred using his old reliable test first. So the doctor took out a railroad pocket watch, and seated across from the woman, the doctor held up the watch and asked her if she could hear the watch's ticking. She said "Sure, just fine." So the doctor got up, walked behind her and asked if she could hear it now. Again she said yes. The doctor then walked across the office and asked if the ticking could still he heard. The woman replied that she heard it easily. Finally, the doctor walked out the door so he was out of sight, and asked if she could still hear the watch. Again the woman said that she heard it clearly. The doctor returned to his chair putting the old watch back in his pocket. Then he looked at the woman and said. "Your hearing is perfect, your problem is not in your hearing; you just don't know how to listen."

We are at times like the woman in this story. We feel so strongly about how things should be in our world that we can't hear what others are saying to us.

I have a friend who is always careful about what he eats. One day he said he went to visit a friend of his who just had triple bypass and he was at home resting. When he got to his friends house he was greeted at the door by his wife. She said, "How great you look you lost so much weight, come in, come in." As he sat and spoke to his friend, his friend's wife said, "Let me make you a sandwich. Is bologna ok?" He said, "No thank you." She said, "Is white bread ok." He again said, "No sandwich please." A few moments later she said, "Would you like mayonnaise or mustard on the sandwich." He said, "No thank you," once again and reminded her that he was on a strict diet. She said, "Well then, how about a piece of cake." He said to me, "This woman heard what I said but she wasn't listening to me."

Jesus is telling the Pharisees in the gospel today that they hear His words but they didn't understand their meaning. They observe the rules but they have forgotten the message in the words, the message of compassion.

Jesus calls us today not just to hear His words but to listen deeply and understand their meaning. He wants us to understand that rules are good but He would rather us be compassionate, loving, patient, and kind to each other. He wants us to listen to the people he sends to us. He wants us to understand what they are saying to us. Some people he sends us are asking to feel accepted by us. Others need to be heard because they are lonely and some just need a word of encouragement from us. Jesus wants us to make allowances for the shortcomings of others; He wants us to be His hands and His voice when we see a person in need.

It is in the simplest things that we show that we are listening to the words of Jesus. Just by spending a little time with a child or friend that needs our attention allows us to bring the love and healing of God to them. Christ calls us to listen to his words for the sake of those we love. Each moment we live we should look for every opportunity to use the talent that God has given us to make His love a living reality for every life we touch.

Every day is a masterpiece

Years ago a sculptor received a block of marble he ordered from the quarry. After examining it carefully, the sculptor rejected the marble because it had a flaw in it. Now this took place long before forklifts were invented, so the workmen had to move the heavy load by using a series of logs to roll the marble. Rather than struggle back to the quarry, one of the men suggested that they take the marble to Michelangelo, who lived down the street. After all, he was known to be a little absentminded. They thought he might not realize that he didn't order a three ton block of marble.

When they arrived Michelangelo inspected the marble; he saw the same flaw that the other sculptor did. But, Michelangelo also saw the block as a challenge to his artistic skills. He couldn't pass it up. Michelangelo proceeded to carve from that seemingly useless block of marble, what is considered to be one of the world's greatest art treasures, the statue of David.

Each morning we get up God presents us with a new day and new situations that are like the block of marble Michelangelo received. They may look a little flawed to us. It is up to us to accept them and make something good of them or we can reject them.

One day I sat in my office and a man came in and began to tell me that he just got a call from his son who was in Europe. He began to say how dissatisfied he was with the way his son turned out. The phone call ruined his day because they had an argument.

To make that day a masterpiece, he should have said to his son thanks for calling. I am so proud of you. The work you do is so important. It's great to hear from you, you made my day. You see he was like the first sculptor; he rejected the marble because it had a flaw, so he gave away the chance to have a masterpiece. We have to be like Michelangelo and accept what comes into our lives and work with it.

In Today's gospel Jesus calls us to the Lenten work of transfiguration. We can transform the coldness, sadness and despair around us into love compassion and hope. The simplest act of kindness can be a dazzling act of transfiguration.

Now God gave us the tools to make every day and everything that comes our way a masterpiece.

- He gave us love so we can overlook the flaws in ourselves and others.

- He gave us a smile to soften the hearts of those around us.

- He gave us understanding so we can accept things the way the are.

- He gave us kindness so; we can feel the goodness of sharing.

- He gave us laughter so we don't take things so serious.

- And He gave us patience so that the gifts He gives us can fold out in all their beauty.

God gave us these tools and placed us in the world as His fellow workers and to be agents of transfiguration. We work with God so that injustice is transfigured into justice, so that there will be more compassion and caring, so that there will be more laughter and joy, so that there will be more togetherness in God's world." As our world is transformed, we too will be transformed and we will never be the same again. We will become God's work of art, His masterpiece.

Don't cheat yourself

A young carpenter married a building contractor's daugh¬ter. One day his father-in-law came to him and said, "I don't want you to start at the bottom of this construction business as I did. I want you to go out to my job-site and build the most tremendous house this town has ever seen. Put the best of everything in it, make it a show¬place, and turn it over to me when you are finished." Well, the boy thought this would be his opportunity to make a killing. So he made a deal with a shady wholesaler and installed sub-standard lumber, shingles, cinder blocks, and cement, but billed for the "best" materials. Then the two cheats split the profits they made.

In a short time the son-in-law presented the keys to the newly finished house to his father-in-law. The father-in-law smiled at the boy and said, "Son did you use the best materials for this tremendous show place?" The boy said yes, (although he knew a good wind would have blown the house over). The father-in-law gave the keys back to the boy and said this is my gift to you and my daughter. I wanted you to live in the best house ever built because I love you both so much. The young man walked away, shattered and frustrated. He thought he was making a fortune at his father-in-law's expense, by shaving money here and there with inferior materi¬als and various shortcuts, but in the end he only cheated himself because of his selfishness.

Sometimes we use inferior materials to build our world by the selfish decisions we make.

About 20 years ago I met a man who told me that he was once was an up and coming manager in the company. He said that in his first year as a manager he was given a large amount of money for bonuses for his group for a job well done. They told him that he could split the money any way he chose with his employees. They said if he felt someone didn't deserve anything he could keep that money for himself. At first he shared the money with the other employees, but as time went on he found excuses to hold back money from them so that he could keep it for himself. He said it wasn't long before the people who worked for him began to slow down in their work and they began to make all kinds of excuses of why they couldn't finish the critical work they were responsible for. He said soon after that he was relieved of his responsibility as manager and was placed in a dead end job. This man lost all he had because of selfishness.

The boy in the story and the man in the example had the chance to make something good out of what they were given but their selfishness destroyed all that they had. Now today we are presented with a gift from God and it's up to us to make it fruitful or not.

God has given each of us a vineyard to care for and the skills to tend it. The vineyard he gave us is the world we live in. In this vineyard we can produce fruits that will help us to have a good and happy life. There are the fruits of compassion, kindness, gentleness, and love growing there and we can use all the fruits that the vineyard produces whenever we want. But there are conditions; God wants us to care for this vineyard and to keep it healthy by making good unselfish decisions. He asks that we share the gifts of our vineyard with the people he sends to us. He may send us a family member, a friend or even an enemy but He requires us to be generous and share the fruits with them. If we do this the vineyard we have will grow and be healthy but if we are selfish we will lose the vineyard.

So what we must do each day to keep the vineyard healthy is to make good quality decisions that benefit all people, not just ourselves. Decisions that help our children grow properly, decisions that set an example of how friendships and relationships should grow. We should share some part of what we have with others. If we do this we will be building a place for ourselves in the Kingdom of God.

How to help others

One day a young man went to visit his spiritual director because of a dream he had the night before. He told the director "I fell into a deep pit. I was helpless and lost hope. I couldn't get out." A man came by and said, "If you can climb up to where I can reach you, I will help you out." A second man came by who studied in the east and said. "You only think you're in a pit." A self-righteous person came along and looked into the pit and said, "Only bad people fall into pits." A person who followed scripture to the letter came by and said, "You must deserve your pit." An IRS agent came along and asked "Are you paying taxes on this pit." There was an optimist who said, "Things could be worse." And a pessimist said, "Things will get worse." Then along came Jesus, who seeing my situation, jumped into the pit with me. He had me climb up on his shoulders and he helped me get out of the pit.

In life we meet many people who have problems and we have two choices. We can stand by the edge and give empty words of wisdom or we get into the pit with them and help them out. When we jump into the pit to help someone through a troubled time it's our way of showing people we are Christians. That's what Jesus wants us to do today in the readings. To be the light of the world you have to live what you believe through action. To be the salt of the earth you must be right into the mix of things, giving flavor to life.

To each person we meet the pit is different. To a person who is homeless, we may say you are able bodied get yourself a job, rather than getting into the pit with them and helping them to put their life together. Some may have an addiction to something. It doesn't have to be drugs, it could be an addition to chocolate or TV. We may say to them you only think you are in need of that thing, rather than getting into the pit and helping them to work through the phases of releasing the habit.

Over the years I have been in the pit myself many times and a lot of people stopped by and give me words of advice. But the people I remember most were those who acted like Jesus and jumped into the pit with me and boosted me out. There was a time I had lost my job and I knew it was my fault. Losing the job was bad enough. I didn't need anyone coming to the pit and trying to bury me with advice. The man who jumped into the pit with me was a Jewish man. He didn't ask how I got there, or why I wasn't trying to get out, or tell me that it was my fault that I was in the pit or worse of all that I deserved the pit. His words were I'll help you get another job. I know a few people who could help you. You don't have to be Catholic to be Christian. Being Christian is a way of life and an attitude for all faiths. It is the definition of a person with good character.

Look for the true gifts

One day a little girl, about kindergarten age, found a little plastic pearl necklace and she thought it was the most beautiful thing she had ever seen. She loved the necklace so much that she wore it everywhere. She wore them to kindergarten, when she went to bed and even when she went out with her mother to run errands. The only time she didn't wear them was in the shower. Each night when bedtime came her father would read her a bedtime story.

One night when he finished the story, her father said to her, "Do you love me?" She said to her father "yes you know I love you." "Well, then he said, give me your pearls." The little girl said "not my pearls!" "You can have Rosie, my favorite doll. Okay?" Her father said "no that's okay" then he kissed her on the cheek and said good night. A week later, her father once again asked after her story, "Do you love me?" "Oh yes, Daddy, you know I love you." "Well, then, give me your pearls" he said. "Oh, Dad, not my pearls take my horse instead." "Do you remember her? She's my favorite." "Her hair is so soft, and you can play with it and braid it and everything." "No, that's okay," he said and brushed her cheek and kissed her good night.

Several days later, when it came time for the bedtime story the little girl's father came into the room and there sat. The little girl sat on the bed with her lip trembling. "Here, Daddy," she said, and held out her hand. She opened it and there was a pearl necklace inside. She placed it into her father's hand. Her father looked at her with a loving smile and took the pearls. Then he reached into his pocket and took out a velvet box and handed it to his daughter. She opened the box and inside was a beautiful set of real pearls.

Sometimes we are like the little girl. We want to hold on to the things in our life to control them. When I began my prayer life years ago, I remember that I would always come to God with a list. If I said three Hail Mary's, I had a name or purpose attached to them. I wanted to make sure that God used them exactly the way I had intended them to be used. Every time I went to pray my list got bigger. And one thing I never did was to ask for something for myself no matter how much I needed anything. Until one day I was so tired of carrying around this list that I decided that I would give my prayers to God as a gift; just like the Magi brought their worldly treasure as a gift to Jesus. I wanted to allow God to do whatever he wanted with the prayers I gave him. As I began to pray a most interesting thing happened, I began to feel good inside and most important, I felt free. I began to realize that at that moment God was giving me the first benefit of my prayers and then he did what he wanted with the rest. It wasn't until that moment that I really began to grow in the spiritual life because I gave God control and he in turn gave me freedom.

Over the years I have brought God many things. I brought him my house and he blessed it and made it a home. I brought him my job and he opened my eyes to see that it was a career. I brought him my friendship and he gave me his love. Today sit for a while and think if there's anything that you have been hanging onto that you might offer to God as a gift. Allow Him to do what He wants with it. Then in your heart approach the crib and present your gift to the child Jesus, just like the Magi did. You may be pleasantly surprised at the blessings He will return to you.

Follow the example

There once was a handsome prince who had a crooked back. This defect kept him from attaining his full potential as the kind of prince he dreamt to be. One day the king had the best sculptor in the land carve a statue of the prince. It portrayed him, however, not with a crooked back but with a straight back. The king placed the statue in the prince's pri¬vate garden. And whenever the prince gazed at it, his heart would quicken.

Months passed, and people began to say, "Do you no¬tice, the prince's back doesn't seem as crooked as it was." When the prince overheard this remark, he gained more confidence in himself. Now he began to spend hours study¬ing the statue and meditating on his personal dream. Then one day a remarkable thing happened. The prince reached high overhead, stretching himself. Suddenly, he was stand¬ing straight and tall, just like the statue.

In the story to king is God the father, the statue of the boy is Jesus, and we are the young prince with a crooked back. God wants us to be holy and he sends us a model, Jesus, to be our guide, to be our example. All we have to do is keep our eye on Jesus and soon we will follow and be like him.

When I was in my forties I had found out how true this little story was. After I had lived my life the way I wanted and it didn't bear the fruits I was looking for I placed Jesus before me as my model. Each day I would get up and do simple things with great care and precision. Even in small things like shaving in the morning. I would take the razor and prepare it with great care and each stroke was done with full concentration slowly. Each thing I did became like the Japanese tea ritual in which each motion is done with the greatest respect. First the sitting position at table then the picking up of the napkin then the placing of the napkin on the lap. Each action was done with great precision and respect for the action. I became less self centered as I took each attribute of Jesus and placed it into my life. Now each day that I looked at the model of Jesus and tried to be like him I noticed that little by little I became a better person.

I never became like him in all things but I did become like him in some. I think we should always hold an ideal and try to fashion ourselves like it each day. I know if we do we will change the world and in the process we will be content with our own lives.

•

The radish

One day a friend of mine told me that he grew up in the city and every time he got the chance he would climb his neighbor's fences and go into their vegetable gardens and pull out the radishes, dust them off and eat them.   His dream was one day to have his own garden where he would grow his own radishes. He didn't know anything about gardening, but that was his dream.

Years later he bought a home and when spring came he was able to plant the radishes he always wanted. He went out and bought some seeds then he turned the soil over, took out all of the weeds, mixed in some fertilizer and then planted the radish seeds perfectly in a row and watered the newly planted seeds. Each morning he would go out and examine the radishes and he would pull out anything that grew where he didn't plant a seed. Weeks passed and he never saw a radish. He asked his neighbor one day why the radishes didn't grow. He said, "I prepared the ground, placed the seeds in the ground with enough room for them to grow and all I saw from time to time was a little weed come up between the radishes, which I pulled out."

His neighbor said, "That's the problem, radishes don't come straight up at first, they grow around the seed. You have been pulling up the radishes not the weeds. Just let them be and they will grow as they should." Life unfolds for us each day and we see new things, situations and people that come into our lives. We don't always understand them or how they will fit in, so we uproot them as though they were weeds and toss them away. When we do that we may be throwing out a blessing from God or an answer to a prayer.

I know a couple who prayed for their daughter to meet someone who would love her and care for her especially when they couldn't be there for her as they got older. So one day she brought home a young boy she liked. When they saw him all they saw was a weed. He was nothing at all like they expected. But in their wisdom they decided to let them be to see what would happen. They thought if it was from God all would be well and if not he would go away. Over time God worked wonders. The young boy became a man and they saw how he loved their daughter and how hard he worked to for her and their grandchildren.

If you wish to see God's work in your lives you need to let things be and watch the outcome rather than how it gets accomplished. Be patient with God and you will see greater gifts then you could have ever imagined.

If you study the lives of the Saints you will find that their first rule is to be patient to see where God is taking them. They traveled the road of blind faith. The most important one who did this was Mary the mother of Jesus. In each step of her life she waited on God, she let each situation take its course at the hand of God. So live by the example of Mary's words of wisdom, and let it be.

Resurrecting the real you

There was a woman who had two sisters and this woman considered herself much plainer then her sisters. Every time she would look in the mirror she was not impressed with what she saw. She would always compare herself to her sisters. Don't get me wrong she was not jealous of her sisters, she loved them very much. This woman was too kind to be jealous. Even the loving kindness that was her special gift from God, she couldn't recognize. One day she met a man who was attracted to her. In the beginning they didn't have much to say to each other; he was a shy person too.

In all of the time they were together she couldn't bring herself to believe that someone would really be interested in her, so she didn't make much of it. This man persisted in coming to visit her and gradually they spent more and more time together. One day he said I love you, and gave her a gentle kiss on the cheek. He said you are so good, you are so wise, you are so sweet.

At first she thought he was joking. But he wasn't. Finally she began to understand, not with her mind but with her heart and this changed her whole world. His words made her see herself in a new way. She looked at herself in the mirror again she saw what this man made her see by the light of his words. She was beautiful, she was lovable, and she was desirable. She was important because this man gave light to her inner beauty; she saw what was hidden to her eyes. She became a new creation. She left what she was behind. You might say she was resurrected.

During Lent we read of a blind man who said to Jesus you can heal me if you want to. Jesus looked at him with love and said I do want to. Then He gave him his sight back and from that moment on he had possibilities. Mary Magdalene considered herself a sinner, an outcast of society until Jesus sparked in her the possibility that she could have the greatest love in her heart. Today I couldn't count the number of churches and statues, there are pointing to her as an example of the love of God.

This is what the life of Jesus is all about. He is God's word of love, a healing love that is free. He was sent by God to give light to what we can be. He shows us the possibilities that are within each and every one of us. He is the light within our hearts that shows us who we are. Just like the man who told the woman that she was lovable, desirable, beautiful and important, so too Jesus comes and lights a spark within our hearts. He shows that we have the possibility to become more then we are today.

Today Jesus looks at us through the eyes of love, and if we just try a little we can see the infinite possibilities in our lives. With a little work who knows what we can become.

Have faith

A very tired traveler came to the banks of a river. There was no bridge there for him to get across this river. It was winter, and the surface of the river was covered with ice. It was getting dark; he wanted to reach the other side while there was enough light to see. He debated about whether or not the ice would hold his weight. Finally, after some time, he got down on his knees and began, very cautiously, to creep across surface of the ice. He thought that by doing this, the ice would be less likely to break under the weight of his body.

After he made his slow and painful journey about halfway across the river, he suddenly heard the sound of singing behind him. Out of the dusk, there came four horses pulling a load of coal and it was driven by a man singing happily, at the top of his lungs, as though he didn't have a care in the world. Here was the traveler, fearfully inching his way on his hands knees. And there, as though without a care in the world, went the driver, his horses, his sled, and the heavy load of coal over the same river.

Many of us go through life lacking faith in the love God has for us. In this story we are the man that is crawling across the ice or the one with the horses pulling the load of coal. The river represents the difficulties that come to us each day of our lives. The ice is God's love for us. The man with the horses has faith and the man who crawls has no faith in God's love.

When we have difficulty come into our lives and we don't feel the love of God, either directly or through our loved ones, we become frightened and can't move, so we crawl or creep through life for fear of thin ice. But when we feel the love of God directly or projected through others we are like the man who sang as he went across the ice with the load of coal. When we feel loved, there is nothing that seems impossible for us to accomplish. There are days we get up and we may feel that no one loves us or cares about us. But that's not true because God loves us no matter what we feel about ourselves or what others think of us. Sometimes we are our own worst enemies, when it comes to love. A person can do the slightest thing to us and we misinterpret it to mean they don't love us. We never turn to God for love. We turn to Him for things.

Jesus tells us today in the Gospel that He loves us very much. He wants us to come to Him when we feel that the load we are carrying in life is too heavy for us. He says "Come to me all you who are burdened and I will give you rest." The rest He gives us is in His love.

I have days where my wife is upset with me, my children or the people I work with. But it is then that I remind myself how much God loves me and I feel strong again. If I know God loves me that's all I need in life to be happy.

When you want to find God, and know how much he loves you, all you have to do is change your routine a little. Turn your attention away from the world or the problem you are facing for a few moments and you will begin to feel the peace and gentleness of His love. Try getting up a few minutes early one morning and step outside your home and look around you. Notice the birds the trees, the flowers and the squirrels. Take a deep breath and begin to feel the peace of God enter your heart. As you see all these things work together you will see your place in creation.

When you feel loved, no matter how many troubles you have, or what body aches you have they will seem to all fade away. The problems and pains don't go away it's just that when you feel loved you gain the strength to overcome them. You will go to work as a person who shares their talents, not like a person who hoards them. You will greet people with an open heart, not with a suspicious nature. You will be more patient with other people and overlook their shortcomings.

When you face rivers of difficulties you do not have to be afraid. You don't have to creep through life. You just have to know you are loved. So pray today that you will feel the love of Jesus in your hearts. Then you will walk with strength and courage through any river of difficulty you may be facing.

The value of a person

A well-known speaker started off his seminar by holding up to $100 bill in a room of about 200 people. Then he asked who would like his $100 bill. The people in the group started putting up their hands. Then he said I'm going to give his $100 bill to one of you, but first, let me do this.

He proceeded to crumple the $100 bill and then he asked who still wants this bill. The people put up their hands once again. Then he said "But what if I do this?" And then dropped on the ground and he started to grind it into the floor with his shoe and as he picked it up the people could see that the bill was all dirty and wrinkled. He asked who still wants this. The people raised their hands once again. The people kept raising their hands because they knew the value of the bill didn't change. No matter what he did to the money it was still worth $100.

In this story we are the $100 dollar bill and the one being asked who wants this bill is God. No matter how many times in our lives we are dropped, crumpled, and ground into the dirt by the decisions we make and the circumstances we place ourselves in, God always wants us. He knows our true value. Not only God, those who love us as well.

One morning, as I was walking to my office I saw a friend at his desk looking a little down. I asked him if there was something I could help him with. He said to me I just got a call from my son. I haven't seen him in over two years. As we talked he told me how much he missed me and loved me. I never thought I would hear those words from him and I thought to myself do I deserve his love with all of the things I did to stop him from growing up with his own choices. And the times I should have been there for him and wasn't.

As this man began to look into himself and reflect on his relationship with his son, he began to see that his choices were the best for the time he lived in. Some were just different and he saw that he could have made some better choices. It is said, "Where there is no reflection there is no life." We are entering the Lenten season and it's a time to reflect on how we lived our lives and the choices we made.

Instead of giving up something or doing something extra during Lent, why not consider giving God ten minutes of your day and reflect on how you lived your life and the choices you have made. This will be a far greater gift you will give God and yourself. When you do this, you will begin to know the lives you touched, the hurting hearts you healed, and the hope that you have brought to others. You will also see the things you could have done better and it is in those times that you must reach out and grow by changing your ways.

If you enter into this Lenten season with an open heart, God will show you your true value and where you need to grow. As you go through this process you may feel as though you are worthless at times. But know this, no matter what has happened or what will happen, whether you are dirty or clean, crumpled or finely creased you are still priceless to God and to the ones who love you. That is the true gift of Lent.

Seeds that grow a good life

There was a woman who was walking through a marketplace, when she saw a sign that said God's fruit stand. She walked over and saw the most perfect fruits she ever laid eyes on. The reddest apples, beautiful peaches. Nectarines twice the size you would expect. God was behind the counter and asked her if he could be of service. She said I would like a bunch of bananas, a dozen perfect apples and three cantaloupes and half dozen perfect peaches. God said "yes, right away, I will be back in a moment." Within two minutes God was back and handed her a bag that was three inches by three inches. The woman opened the bag and looked inside and said, "Where are all the fruits I ordered?" He said "they're in the bag." She said "but these are just seeds." God said "I know that's all I sell. Plant them and care for them and they'll grow to be what you want."

I believe that just before the moment we are born, we stop at God's fruit stand. In those few seconds, God puts a packet of seeds on the shelf in our hearts. Within that packet there are enough seeds for the life we will live. But it's up to us to take the seeds and plant them. Now the seeds God puts there are not for growing apples, bananas, or cantaloupes but they are there for us to become carpenters, musicians, doctors, lawyers. There are also are seeds there that improve the inner quality of our lives like compassion, patience, kindness, friendship, courage, perseverance, forgiveness and love.

When we are young, God gives us a preview of each of the seeds or talents He has given us. It's like walking through a supermarket and in isle one you get a sample of pizza. Isle two you can taste fruit and in isle three you can have a cookie. God gives his previews in the education we get in school and also from our families.

I remember when I was in school one of the courses I took was woodworking. I remember the first project I worked on; it was a small box you could store papers in. I learned how to cut the wood without splitting it, then I used a plane to make the wood even and then I sanded it to make it smooth. Once the wood was ready, I glued the box together and dried it overnight. Then it was ready for the final finish to be put on. In this small project God was letting me know that I had the ability to do carpentry. All I had to do was to choose to be a carpenter and then work at it.

As I said, school is not the only place that we can have this preview of our talents. We also get them from our families. I work with a young woman, who this past Christmas got a sewing machine. She told me that when she was a little girl her mother used to make matching outfits for her and her sister. She never placed any real importance on what her mother did, but now that she received this gift, she began to think back to watching and helping her mother sewing these outfits. Now she makes time on the weekends to make new dresses. She is getting so good at it, I can never tell if she bought the dresses or made them. When we see a preview of some of the possibilities we have within us, it becomes our choice to use these talents or not. The hardest part of planting is having patience and perseverance waiting for the results to appear.

In the Gospel message today, God is tells us not to worry about time. He just asks us to scatter the seeds he has given us. The seeds he gives us are those talents that will bring about the kingdom of God. Whenever we us these talents we benefit our community as well as our own families. Each time a carpenter seed is planted a house is built. When a doctor seed is planted a life is saved, when someone plants an engineer seed, a bridge is built, and when a priest seed is used a soul is healed. When we plant these seeds and work at them we show those around us how to take responsibility and live as responsible people, especially the young people in our lives.

One thing I have learned is that it is never too late to develop the talents God has given us. You know if you take a seed and put it on a shelf and leave it there for two years you will come back and still find the seed sitting on the shelf, unchanged. If you plant it in the ground the seed will begin to grow no matter how long it has been on that shelf.

I ask you today to take some time and pray to God that he will help you remember the previews he gave you of your talents when you were in school or living at home with you family. If you are young these previews will help you make proper decisions as your life unfolds. If you are older, they can become hobbies or maybe even a small business that you always wanted.

Plant one seed at a time and work at it a little at a time and see where it leads you. You know God is our Father and he has made sure we have all of the things we need to live a happy life. So take a moment today and say thank you Father for these seeds of life.

Working together

One day a group of people were taking a tour of the California's giant Sequoia trees. The people were amazed at how huge the trees were. The guide said the sequoias were the oldest trees known to man. Some were 3 to 4 thousand years old. And they are the tallest in the entire world, the largest measuring 367 feet high and 83 feet around the base. Finishing the tour, the guide said the giant Sequoia trees have their roots just barely below the surface of the ground. Just as he said that a man hollered out "That's impossible! I'm a country boy, and I know that if the roots don't grow deep into the earth, strong winds will blow the trees over." The guide said to him, "No Sir, not Sequoia trees. They grow only in groves and their roots intertwine under the surface of the earth. So, when the strong winds come, they hold each other up."

When we commit ourselves to a relationship we are like the giant Sequoia that grow a system of strong roots, and it is those roots that we share that hold us together, when the winds of life become too strong for us to stand alone. Now the roots that connect us are the little things in life we share or see in each other that we love.

Forty-nine years ago I married to my wife Hannah. As I look back it was the best decision I ever made. But there were times for the both of us that we wanted to go out for a loaf of bread and come back a year later. I think we all feel that way sometimes.

But as I looked back, I could see that it's the little things in life that made our marriage strong. When I think of the way she looked on our wedding day, and the happiness I saw in her face and the happiness in my heart the moment she said I do, to be my wife, that's one of those little roots of love. When I remember that she can't say the word aluminum or linoleum and when she would try we would laugh. Or the times when we go to bed after an argument and in the morning I see her asleep and I am filled with love for her. In that moment, God made me remember all of the good things my wife has ever done for me. I realize how much I love her and how lucky I am.

You see, God uses those little roots of love to remind us of how much we love one another so that when things get tough, we are able to stand together against the winds of life, just like the giant Sequoias. Love is the glue that holds all things together in God's creation and makes everything strong.

As it was for Hannah and me, so it will be for anyone who enters into a relationship. So, remember the little things in life, and allow God to remind you each day through them of how much you love each other and how you depend on each other as you travel the road of life together.

Understanding God's ways

There was a farmer who owned an old mule. The mule was free to roam his property as he pleased. One day the mule went near the old abandoned barn and as he moved around the barn he fell into the old well that had dried up. The farmer heard the mule crying and he came to look to see what happened. After carefully assessing the situation, the farmer got a few neighbors and when they returned they began to throw dirt into the well.

The old mule became hysterical because he thought the farmer was trying to bury him. With each shovel full of dirt that landed on the mule's back he got more hysterical. Then the mule realized that as the dirt landed on his back he shook it off and then when it went under his feet he noticed that he stepped up higher. As each shovel full of dirt hit the mule's back, he would say to himself "shake it off and step up". No matter how painful the blows or distressing the situation seemed the old mule fought "panic" and just kept right on shaking it off and stepping up!

It wasn't long before the old mule, battered and exhausted, stepped triumphantly out of the well! What seemed to be sure to bury him actually saved him.

We are the mule and God is the farmer. God sees us in a predicament and he tries to help us but we think He is trying to bury us deeper in our problems or take away what little comfort we have. That's what happened in the Gospel reading today. John said repent or change your ways but the Pharisees thought that he came to take away what little comfort they had.

As human beings we need new things to come into our life. That's what makes life for us and helps us to mature. But within ourselves we are afraid to change and incorporate these new things, because like the Pharisees we have gotten comfortable and don't want the pain that change brings.

I knew a man who used to drink a little too much. He enjoyed it but he didn't notice that his friends seemed to be getting more distant. He didn't notice that his raises weren't as good as they used to be and he didn't notice that his children were falling behind in their grades. One day this man saw the affect his habit was having on his life and he decided to change his life.

This man admitted that he had a problem and the he bore the pain of the cure. He was like the mule in the story.

This man had terrible pain as he made the journey of repentance. He didn't think he had a friend in the world and he couldn't see God in his life. But by doing what the mule did he shook off the pain, embarrassment and the feeling of being alone by putting it beneath him. And each day he stepped up a little higher until he walked triumphantly out of the well of alcohol addiction.

John the Baptist is sent by God to tell us to repent or change our lives. But in order to repent we must look at the way we live and the things we have done and see how we have treated people in our past. When we do this we will find that each of us have something that we need to repent from. It may be that we don't listen to others because we are too self centered. It may be that we get involved too much in the lives of others. It could be anything we do to extreme that we have gotten comfortable with. Repentance or change brings with it some discomfort within us. But to overcome this, remember the mule and say "Shake it off and step up." I assure you in no time you will walk out of the habit that holds you prisoner. Pray to God for strength and make the changes in your life just a little at a time. Remember God doesn't expect you to make changes like this quickly, they take time.

The value of truth

There is an old Indian story about a 12 year old boy who died of a snake bite. The poison took away his life. His grieving parents took his body to the holy man in the village and laid it before him. The three of them sat around the body sadly for a long time. Then the father rose and went to the boy and placed his hands on the boy's feet and said "In all of my life I have not worked for my family as I should have." The poison left the feet of the child. The mother then rose and stretched her hands over the boy's heart and said "I have not loved my family as I should have." And the poison left the heart of the child. The holy man rose and went to the boy and placed his hands over the boys head and said "In all my life I have not believed or had faith in the words I have spoken." The poison left the head of the child. The child rose up, the parents and the holy man roes up, and the village rejoiced that day.

This boy represents humanity; the human family. The three things that were mentioned by the parents and the holy man are the three things that destroy humanity. Not using the proper work ethic, not loving the human family as brothers and sisters and not believing in God and each other. These are the destroyers of the human family. In each action we perform in life we either lift up humanity or take it down. We add to it or take away from it. Humanity will grow or decline not because of any huge thing we accomplish but because of the small things we do.

Norman Vincent Peal tells of a boy who when he was 8 years old, witnessed his father, who was preparing his income taxes, altering the figures. His father said its OK son everybody does it. When he was 16 he worked in a supermarket. His job was to put the overripe strawberries on the bottom of the basket. The manager said its OK kid everybody does it. When he was 19 he was approached by a student who offered him the test results for the class he was taking for $50. The student said its OK everybody does it. Eventually he was caught and sent home in disgrace from school. His parents questioned where he had learned these things. Well he learned them by example. When we know what we should do and we don't do it, we affect the whole human family. You never know who is watching and what they will do with what they see.

When I shop with my wife I pick up the products that fell on the floor. She would tell me not to pick them up and to let the people who work there do it. I still pick them up but after a few years I notice that she started to pick up some of the things others dropped on the floor. You see we have an effect on humanity and the way it acts.

When I don't walk 10 extra feet to park my car properly and choose to block a driveway or ignore a sign, humanity takes a step back. When drugs are abused, humanity takes a step back. When too much alcohol is taken, humanity takes a step back and when we take fistfuls of napkins in a fast food restaurant because we think no one is watching that's a step back for the human family.

Humanity grows when we make time for our family or when we do the best job we can and set good example. Michael Angelo was painting in the Sistine chapel. One morning and he was painting in the furthest corner and a person walked by and said to him "Michael Angelo why are you painting there so carefully who will know." His answer was "I will know." If he would have taken the shortcut he eventually would have taken other shortcuts and then we would not have benefited from this great artist's work.

The human family grows in the way we walk and talk. It grows in the way we carry ourselves, our courage, our honesty, our moderation and respect for each other. When we encounter humanity the first person we meet and who benefits is ourselves, then our family and friends and then all people.

So remember all of us must do the very best we can in our work; to love as deeply as we can this human family of ours and to trust each other and have faith in the one who loves us, God. So do the right thing for the sake of humanity.

Holding life together

One day a spider began to build a huge web. He thought to himself that it would be a masterpiece. He began by lowering himself on the finest and the strongest thread he could make. You know a spider can manufacture several different types of silk thread. Once in position he began to build his web. When the web was done the beauty of this web began to attract other spiders. They would stop and admire it, as the most beautiful piece of work they had ever seen.

The web was so beautiful that a nearby school in the area would take the children to see the web for its sheer beauty. They say in the evening you could see the spider sitting on the top of his web and he would rub his little hands and legs together with great satisfaction.

One day the spider decided to check his web and make a few improvements. As he was making his rounds he looked at the thread that he began the web with and thought to himself that this thread was old and there were so many other threads that looked more beautiful. He said to himself, I don't need this anymore. He decided to cut this thread away. He began to chew on the thread and as he took the final bite the web came crashing down like a bubble in cold water.

There are times we are like the spider cutting the line that holds our life together.

Today this Gospel reading is one from the last supper. It is placed here today because it is a reminder of the promise that Jesus had made to us. The promise is important but we tend to forget it. Jesus says if you remember my words the Father and I will make our home with you and further more I will send the Holy Spirit to remind you of my words and instruct you in everything. You might say that this promise that Jesus makes us today is like the thread that the spider made to start his web. It is the strongest and most important connection we have as we spin the web we call life. But even with all of the reminders I still forget the promise.

Let me give you an example, the other day at work I was sitting with a friend and he asked me how I get encouragement at the office. You see we share a common problem. Our managers are in the city and we only hear from them once a month if we are lucky. Every so often we get an envelope from them or a call when they want something, but for the most part we are left to ourselves. I began to answer his question by saying I get my encouragement from the employees or my wife or other people in the building. But then, I said that is not true. The only encouragement I get is in the morning when I get up and sit and read some scripture or look out the window at the trees and then God begins to speak to me in my mind and my heart. He shows me the things I did and I begin to know that I have done my best. Then after a while He will show me the next logical step in a project. By the time I get to work I feel good. I have the encouragement to continue. My encouragement comes from God.

That's not the first time I had forgotten God in my life. When I was younger I remember teaching my children how to build model rockets. It would take me a few weeks. I had to explain everything to them. I had to show them how important detail was and patience. When I was finished, we looked at it and said how beautiful it was. I thought to myself boy you are you good. I had forgotten the thread that made it happen; I forgot who gave me the skill to do the work. I forgot who provided the patience, who gave me the opportunity and who gave me the children.

I was just like the spider. I had forgotten God's commitment to me and how much a part of my life He is. I began to think that the work I had done was all mine and that God had nothing to do with it. It is very important to realize that we all have three permanent house guests living in our hearts.

And their promise to us is that they are there to help us and to be a part of our lives. If you are a young person remember to include God in all of your life and relationships. Remember He gives you talents and opportunities. If you are older and established in life take time to renew your relationship with God and be sure you include Him in your projects and relationships. And if you are older still sit and enjoy the work you have done together with God and say thank you. All of us at times find ourselves forgetting that God is with us. But it's never too late to renew that relationship.

Develop a deep relationship

There were three seers who were encouraged by their people to find a cave that was called "The cave of wisdom and life." The cave was a long way off and it was a hard journey for them to make. The seers wanted to please their people and so they made preparations for this challenging and arduous journey. They traveled for many days and finally they saw the cave in the distance. As they moved closer they saw how big and dark the cave looked and there at the entrance of the cave was a guard. As they moved closer the guard said to them, "You cannot enter the cave until you answer one question for me. But before you answer it you must discuss the question with each other. Then I will provide a proper guide to take you through the regions of the cave." One of the seers asked, "Well what is your question?" The guard said, "How far into the cave of wisdom and life do you wish to go?" The three seers talked it over as the guard suggested and then they came back to the guard. The oldest seer said "Not very far. We just want to go far enough into the cave so that we can say we had been there." The guard watched disappointed as the three seers walked a bit into the cave and then turned and went home.

In the story Jesus is the guard, we are the seers and the cave is our heart within us. All of us are asked today by Jesus "How far into the cave do you wish to go? Or how deep do you want your relationship with me to be?"

Many years ago I had to make the choice of how deep a relationship I was going to have with Jesus. I had to make some difficult choices and then live by those decisions. I asked the question, will there be danger? Will I be asked to do something that I would rather not do? Will I have to change or give up something that I am comfortable with? The answer to all of those questions was yes. You see I realized that to enter into a deep relationship with Jesus, my life was going to change. I would not be first anymore. At first I was afraid to make the commitment, but I realized that I had to have faith in the guide. I decided to move forward with trust. At first it was a little tough, I had to talk less and listen more. I had to concentrate and focus on all that I did one thing at a time, trusting that Jesus would watch out for me. Previously, all I had to do is watch out for was myself. As time went on I began to see how nice it was to see others do well.

When I started on this journey, I would use people and love things. Over time I learned that I should love people and use things. You see when you enter into a deep relationship with Jesus the whole world changes. Today in the Gospel, Jesus extends the invitation for us to enter into a deep relationship with Him

Balancing God and the world

Two young men met in college and became friends. One wanted to be a businessman and the other a farmer. When they graduated they went their separate ways. Years later, the farmer was visiting New York and before he left he wanted to see how his old friend was doing, so he called and made arrangements to meet for lunch. They met in the businessman's office at Rockefeller Center and they talked about old times. When it came close to noontime, the businessman said "Let's go to one of the restaurants close by." As they were walking down 5th Avenue the farmer stopped and said to his friend, "did you hear that?' His friend said "Hear what?" The farmer said "The cricket, don't you hear it?" His friend said, "All I hear is the sound of the cars blowing their horns and the people talking." The farmer walked over to a planter on the side of the building and he pulled out a little cricket and showed it to his friend. The businessman said, "How were you able to hear a cricket with all this noise?" The farmer said, "It all depends on what you're taught to hear." With that, the farmer reached into his pocket and took out a hand full of coins and threw them down on the sidewalk, and as they hit the ground all the people on the street stopped. The farmer said it's what you are taught to hear. I was taught to hear the cricket and they were taught to hear the coin.

The cricket is the presence of God and the coins are the material things in life. We must have a balance between God and material things in order to live a proper life.

The rich man in the Gospel reading today forgot what was important. He forgot because he was centered only on the material part of life. He only saw himself and not the people around him or the community. If he had opened his heart to allow God in, he may have said, "I have enough things so instead of building new barns I will share some of this wealth with others. Then his heart would have been filled with peace." And the two men that asked Jesus to settle their argument were willing to ruin their family relationship rather than share their inheritance. They forgot their family history and how much they meant to each other.

When we concentrate on the things of the world we become filled with greed and selfishness. We begin to use people and love things instead of loving people and using things. In each thing we do we need to invite God to be with us. It's OK to have cars and boats and nice homes but take moment and say thank you God. When you invite God to be with you, God opens your heart to share your gifts, not hoard them. Where God is, greed and selfishness give way to charity and love. We can't just be with God and we just can't be with the things of the world. When the cricket and the coin live in balance we see a wider and deeper view of life and we experience our part in it. Look In your heart today and see if there are places that you can invite God to be with you, and then the cricket and the coin will be in balance for you.

The sacrifices of others

There was a boy who was constantly coming home late from school. Now there was never a good reason for the boy being late and no amount of discussion seemed to help. Finally in desperation the boy's father sat him down and said "The next time you come home late from school you are going to be given bread and water for supper, and nothing else. Is that clear son?" The boy looked into the fathers eyes and nodded. The boy understood perfectly.

A few days later the boy came home even later than usual from school. The boy's mother met him at the door but didn't say anything to him. His father met him in the living room and he also said nothing to the boy. That night when they sat down at the table for dinner the boy's heart sank down to his feet. His father's plate was filled with food and his mother's plate was filled with food. But on his plate there sat one lonely piece of bread and in front of the plate there was a small glass of water. The boy first stared at the bread and then at the water. He thought to himself this was the punishment that my parents promised me. To make things worse he was especially hungry that night. The father waited for the full impact to sink in. Then he quietly took the boy's plate and placed it in front of himself and he took his own plate and placed it in front of the boy. The boy understood what his father was doing. His father was taking upon himself the punishment that the boy brought on himself by his behavior.

Years later he recalled the incident and said "all my life I have known what God is like because of what my father did that night by taking my punishment on himself."

The father in this story loves his son so much that he will bear his pain. When someone we love, or care about makes a decision that may draw them away from the safe road of life, we also bear the pain. As they make their decision, they don't seem to feel the pain or understand the consequences. But we who love them feel the pain every minute of the day while they are on the road they have chosen. Our hearts are not at rest until they are safe home on the right path again.

One day a man told me of something that happened to him and his son. It seemed his son was having a terrible time in school; it was so terrible for him that he wanted to quit school. He thought that he could do better learning his lessons directly from his life experiences. This one day he went to his father and said "Dad I want to leave school and find a different way in life." His father protested and said "I have worked so hard for you to have this opportunity and you are going to throw it away?" Eventually the father gave in and signed the boy out of school. It nearly broke his heart. The boy went out found a job and started a family. Then he needed a second job and then one on weekends. After a few years he realized that his father was right. He placed his self pride aside and went back to school.

It's not always easy for us to come back home and admit that the decision we made was not good for us. It takes a lot of soul searching, determination. And we must admit to ourselves this may have been the wrong choice for us.

Once we come back we need two things; first, the forgiveness of the ones we may have hurt, if not in person then within our hearts, and second, we need the ability to forgive ourselves.

If we know the pain we suffer when someone we love makes a decision that may hurt them, what do you think God feels. God the Father lives in our hearts and we are His prodigal children. He sits in our hearts and waits for us to come home after we make the journey into our choices. Our lives contain choices that are loving choices and selfish choices. When we make a loving choice the whole community is in harmony. When we make a selfish choice the community suffers separation. But it is, in fact we who have separated ourselves from the community. God takes on the burden of our selfish choices just like the father in the story, who switched plates with his son. And the father who allowed his son to quit school and didn't take away his choice but stood waiting for the day when he would come home to him or come to his senses. Love is a very joyous thing and it is also very painful. Without freedom there can be no love. Once we allow someone we love to make a choice that we don't think is good for them we can only walk with them in their decision and be there for them when they stumble or need help.

Take some time today and look at some of the choices you have made. See if they build the human family or separate it. And then see if you can come home to those you have been separated from. Don't forget the most important thing of all is to forgive yourself, because everyone else has already forgiven you.

Excess can hold us back

One day a fox was walking through the forest when he came to a tree that looked like it was hollowed out in the center. The fox moved closer, looked inside and found a large quantity of food that had been stored there. Although it was a tight squeeze, he fit himself in and he began to eat all of the food in the tree. There was so much food there that he wasn't able to finish it all. So he rested for a while and then he tried to get out of the tree but all he was able to do was get his head out because he had eaten so much. The next morning the fox sat there with his head out of the tree. Just at that time, another fox was passing by so he told the fox his story and then asked him to help him out of the tree. But the other fox said to him I can't help you. You must help yourself. Stop eating for a while until your stomach gets smaller and then you will be able to get out. The fox had to choose his priorities. He had to stop eating or lose his freedom. Food is a good thing but not if it is done to excess as the fox found out.

Sometimes we are like the fox. We find something good and become attached to it. Before you know it, it is in control of us and we lose our freedom.

Let me give you an example. A few years ago I would get up early in the morning and read a little scripture passage. Then I would say a rosary. Then I would go to Mass. One day while at mass I found a small prayer to St. Jude. I liked it and then began to say it every day. I just kept accumulating prayers until there was so many I didn't have time to talk to my wife in the morning and worst of all I didn't leave room for God to talk to me. What began with peace and joy ended controlling me and my life. I had forgotten what was important. Prayer is good but not if we neglect the other things that are important to God, like family or work.

Today, Jesus went into the desert and was tempted not by anything bad but with things that are good. Jesus was tempted to be ruler of the kingdoms of the world. If He were a king he could take sorrow away from those He ruled. He could have taken a piece of bread, a thing so small who could deny it to Him. The devil tried to change His priorities but Jesus didn't let him. The devil said put yourself first, not God. But Jesus placed His gifts at the Father's disposal.

The devil tempts good people with temptations of goodness not of bad things. It is very difficult to get a good person to do a bad thing. But the devil thinks if he gives us enough good things to do we will get confused in our priorities and then begin to grow away from God.

This is the way the devil works. He says work a few hours extra it's good for your family. Then the work becomes a habit and the thing that helped your family now takes you away. Your priority was your family and now its work. You begin to do a little exercise and the devil says the more you do the better you will feel and look. You exercise so much that the devil gets you to forget that your priority is life, not exercise. The devil says one doughnut is good, but three is better. Too much of a good thing is bad.

During Lent we are called upon to do the same thing Jesus did. He went into the desert and put aside all of the things of this world and then He organized His priorities. He chose God first. During Lent we must leave the world behind and go in the desert to ask the question. Are the gifts God has given us been used for God's purposes or have they been used for other purposes?

No one is exempt from answering this question. The little fox had to go into the desert within himself. He had to place the food aside. It wasn't easy for him, but if he was to be free he had to do it. I went into the desert within myself. I placed my prayers aside, that wasn't easy for me, then picked them up one at a time and started over. It helped me to make more room for my family and God in my life. Pray to Jesus today, as we begin our Lenten journey, to help us to set our priorities so we choose God's will in our lives.

Planting the seeds of a good life

Once there was a good king who ruled wisely and was loved by all the people of his kingdom. One day the king called his four daughters together and told them that he was leaving on a long journey. He said, "In my absence I am leaving the four of you in charge of my kingdom. But before I leave, I wish to give each of you a gift." It is my prayer that this gift will help you learn how to rule." The king placed a single grain of rice in each daughter's hand. Then he left on his journey. The oldest daughter immediately went to her room. She tied a long golden thread around the grain of rice and placed it in a beautiful crystal box. Every day she picked up the box and looked at it. The second daughter also went to her room, where she placed the grain of rice in a wooden box and put it in a secure spot under her bed. The third daughter looked at the grain of rice and thought, "This grain of rice is no different from any other grain of rice." She simply threw the grain of rice away. The youngest daughter took her grain of rice to her room and wondered about the significance of the gift. She wondered for a week, then a month. When nearly a year passed, she understood the meaning of the gift. For several years the four daughters ruled their father's kingdom.

Then one day, the king returned. The king greeted each of his daughters, and then asked to see the gifts he had left with them. The oldest daughter rushed to her room and brought back the crystal box. "Father," she said, "I carefully tied a golden thread around the grain of rice and have kept it near my bed where I have looked at it every day since you left." The king accepted the box and said "Thank you." The second daughter presented her father with a wooden box containing the grain of rice. "All these years I've kept the rice secure under my bed," she said. "Here it is." The king accepted the box, and said, "Thank you." The third daughter rushed into the kitchen, found a grain of rice, ran back and said, "Father, here is my grain of rice." The king smiled and accepted the grain of rice, and said, "Thank you." Finally the youngest daughter stepped before her father and said, "I do not have the grain of rice that you gave me," she said. "Well, what have you done with it?" the king asked. "Father, I thought about that grain of rice for nearly a year before I discovered the meaning of the gift. I realized that the grain of rice was a seed. So I planted it in the ground. Soon it grew, and from it I harvested other seeds. I then planted all those seeds, and again I harvested the crop. Father, I've continued to do this. Come outside, look at the results." The king followed his daughter where he looked out at an enormous crop of rice stretching as far as the eye could see. There was enough rice to feed the entire kingdom. The king took off his golden crown and placed it on her head, and from that day on, the youngest daughter ruled the kingdom.

When we come into this world we are given a gift from God, it is the gift of wisdom. It is like the little seed that the king gave his daughters. But for the seed to grow it must be planted in the fertile ground of a grateful and thankful heart.

When we have a grateful heart we see all of life differently. Before I understood this seed called wisdom I would always make quick decisions not thinking of the pros or cons of what I was doing. I remember when I was in junior high school it was mandatory to take a foreign language. So I chose French. My father told me that it would come in handy someday; God doesn't give you a gift that you will not need someday or a problem that doesn't make you stronger. But I said without thinking what does my father know. After the first year I forgot about what I had learned, I tossed my notes aside. When I was about 35 I had to take an emergency business trip to Paris and of course I had forgotten everything I learned in school. I can't tell you how embarrassed I was standing in front of the hotel holding my money out in my hand and having the cab driver just take what he wanted. Had I sat for a moment with a grateful heart, God would have shown me the meaning of the gift and how it would be useful later in life.

When you have a grateful heart you open up to God and He speaks to you and lets you know the true value of a person or event that you have been just presented with. You see gratefulness opens your heart to see goodness and purpose and that is wisdom. That's why Jesus gives us this Gospel example today. Those who have oil have used the gift of wisdom and it gave light to them. And those who waited to get oil were those who never used the gift of wisdom and it caused them to miss out on life.

Remember the gift of wisdom is a seed. It will be of no use to you if you put it in a box for safekeeping and take it out and look at it once in a while. Wisdom is of no use to you if you toss it aside. Wisdom will only grow if you plant it in the fertile ground of a grateful and thankful heart and apply it to all you do.

The rewards of a good life

High above the city, on a tall column, stood a statue of the happy prince. He was gilded with thin leaves of fine gold. His eyes were two fine sapphires and on his sword there was a beautiful ruby. The town council thought the statue of the happy prince brought honor to the town. One night a swallow flew over the city. His friends had gone south six weeks before, but he had been delayed. As he arrived in the city he looked for a proper place to stay. When he saw the statue of the prince, he decided to take shelter between his feet. As he made himself comfortable he placed his head under his wing and settled in for the night. As he began to doze off he felt a drop of water hit his wing. He looked up in the sky and saw that not a cloud was there. He made himself comfortable again and in a few seconds another drop of water came down on him. This time when he looked up he saw the face of the happy prince and he noticed that he had tears coming down his golden cheeks. The swallow was filled with pity and asked "who are you"? "I am the happy prince." "Why are you weeping then?" asked the swallow. "When I was alive I lived in a palace where sorrow was not allowed to enter. I played with my friends in the day and at night I would lead the great ball. I never saw misery in my life. When I died I was placed here on this pedestal and I now see the misery in the city. Although my heart is made of lead, I can't choose but to weep.

The prince said to the swallow, far away I see a little street there is a poor house. One of the windows is open and I can see a woman seated at a table. Her face is thin and worn, and she has coarse, red, hands all torn by a needle, for she is a seamstress. In a bed in the corner of the room her little boy is lying ill. He has a fever and is asking for some oranges. His mother has nothing to give him but river water and so he is crying. The prince said to the little swallow "will you take the ruby from my sword and bring it to the woman. You see my feet are fastened to this pedestal and I cannot move." The swallow said "my friends are waiting for me in the south I don't see how I can do this." Once again the prince spoke and said "Little swallow, will you stay with me for one night and be my messenger. This boy is so thin and the mother is so sad". The prince looked so sad that it made the swallow feel sorry and even though it was very cold the swallow said "I will stay with you for one night and be your messenger." Thank you, thank you said the prince. The swallow picked up the ruby from his sword and began his journey over the city. He came to the house and the boy was tossing feverishly on his bed; the mother had fallen asleep. He placed the great ruby on the table next to the woman's thimble. Then he flew gently around the bed fanning the boy's forehead with his wings. "How cool I feel said the boy. I must be getting better." Then he sank into a peaceful sleep.

The swallow returned to the prince and told him what he had done. The little swallow said to the prince "It's curious, I feel quite warm now, although it's quite cold." That's because you have done a good deed said the prince. The prince continued through the night sending the little swallow first to a student who needed money for fire wood and food, then to a little girl who was begging in the street. All night long the swallow moved about the city at the prince's direction. Taking a sapphire here, a gold leaf there, until the morning when the statue had nothing more to give and the little swallow had no more strength.

The swallow said to the prince please let me kiss your hand because I must go now. The prince said to the swallow "I am glad you are going south to be with your friends, you have stayed too long here with me, but you must kiss me on the lips for I love you." The little swallow kissed the prince and then fell to the ground and at that moment there was a great crack that sounded within the prince as though something had broken. The fact is that the sound was the lead heart within the prince that had broken in two.

In the morning the mayor of the city and the town council had made their way to the top of the hill to see the statue and when they looked they saw a statue that looked a little more than a beggar. The mayor said look how terrible he looks his ruby is gone and the sapphires he had for eyes are no longer there and all of the gold leaves are gone. Look there is a bird that has died at his feet. What a disgrace he said. They had the statue taken down and melted except for the heart. They say that no matter how hot they made the furnace the broken heart would not melt. They threw it on a dust heap where the swallow was also lying.

One day God said to one of his angels "Bring me the two most precious things in the city." The angel brought him the lead heart and the little swallow. You have rightly chosen said God, for in my garden of paradise the little bird shall sing forever and the happy prince shall be at my side.

Within each of us live a prince and a swallow. The prince has in his possession gifts for the world we live in and the swallow is the messenger. We may call the prince Jesus, Abraham, David, Spirit, God or conscience. But no matter what we call him he is the one who holds the gifts within our hearts. These gifts are for our children when they need someone to listen to them. They are for our spouses to give them our encouragement and appreciation. We use them in the office when we do our work. The power of the gifts never diminishes.

There is one thing that needs to be done in order to use these gifts. We need to set free the little swallow in our hearts and become the messengers for the prince so that this world can benefit from these gifts. Pray today that we listen and hear the voice of the prince within us and for the strength to release the swallow to become the messenger to the world we live in.

Moving from bad to good

There's an old European story about a traveler who came upon a barn where the devil had stored seeds that he planned to sow in the hearts of people. There were bags of seeds variously marked "Hatred," "Fear," "Lust," "Despair," "Un-forgiveness," "Envy," "Greed," "Drunkenness."

Out from the shadows, the devil appeared and struck up a conversation with the traveler. He was happy to tell the traveler how easily the seeds sprouted in the hearts of men and women everywhere. He pointed to the seeds of fear and said, when these seeds grow they paralyze a person so they cannot make any decisions, in every way they turn they become unsure of themselves in all they do.

Envy and greed are good because they cause families and friends to separate. Just look at what happens when a family has to share an inheritance. This seed also helps hatred to grow stronger. Drunkenness is a favorite of mine because it causes people to speak at the wrong times and this too causes separation; that helps the seed of un-forgiveness to grow strong.

Each seed is special and as it grows it brings with it separation from God and people. The devil was so proud of his work. "Tell me," the traveler asked, "are there any hearts in which these seeds will not sprout?" Looking at the traveler carefully, the devil slyly confessed, "These seeds will never sprout in the heart of a kind, gener¬ous, thankful and joy filled person.

When we do good things the seeds of sin and temptation stop growing within our hearts. I know a man who always began the Lenten season by making a list of things that needed to improve within him. When the list was done he would pick one thing and then struggle with it for 40 days trying to conquer it. He rarely succeeded and all the other things that needed to be improved would never get worked on.

Then one Lenten season he prepared his list in the usual way and then he threw the list in the garbage. He decided to do at least one good thing each day during the 40 day period.

He used to get requests for donations in the mail each week and he would always throw them into the garbage. But during these 40 days he began to send them each a little something. It wasn't much. Sometimes just a dollar but he never declined anyone. This made him feel right within himself. His confidence and self-esteem began to grow. As this happened he began to do more good things. He did things like letting someone who was behind him in the supermarket with only one or two items go in front of him. He held the door open for strangers. The more good he did the better he felt. The better he felt, the better he did in his work. The better he did in his work, the more he placed in the donation envelope. Before long the list of shortcomings didn't matter, anymore because he became a new person, a good person.

In the Gospel today, Jesus it tempted by the devil three times. But each time he digs into his store of goodness and pushes the temptation aside. During the Lenten season I ask you to toss away your list of shortcomings and be resolved to do something good each day. This Lent can be a time in which we can change our world for the better. This will help push the darkness of the devil away. Take some time today and think if there something good you can do to make this world a better place, and if there is, make that your gift to God. Then when Easter morning comes you will be a new person, a good person.

Being a reflection of the Creator

A Greek philosopher and teacher ended a lecture asking, "Are there any questions?" A young man spoke up and asked "What is the meaning of life?" There was the usual laughter you might expect when a question like this is asked.

The professor looked into the eyes of the student for a long time trying to see how serious the boy was about the question he asked. Then the professor answered "I will answer your question." Then taking his wallet out of his hip pocket, he fished into it and brought out a very small, round mirror, about the size of a quarter.

Then he said, 'When I was a small child, during the war, we were very poor and we lived in a remote village. One day, on the road, I found several broken pieces of a mirror from a wrecked motorcycle. I tried to find all the pieces and put them together, but it was not possible, so I kept only the largest piece, this one.

By scratching it on a stone I made it round. I began to play with it as a toy and became fascinated by the fact that I could reflect light into dark places where the sun would never shine in deep holes and crevices. It became a game for me to get light into the most inaccessible places I could find.

I kept the little mirror, and as I went about growing up, I would take it out in idle moments and continue the challenge of the game. As I became a man, I grew to understand that this was not just a child's game but an example for what I might do with my life. I came to understand that I am not the light or the source of light. But light, truth, understanding, and knowledge are there, and they will only shine in many dark places if I reflect it.

'I am a fragment of a mirror whose whole design and shape I do not know. Nevertheless, with what I have, I can reflect light into the dark places of this world into the black places in the hearts of men and change some things in some people. Perhaps others may see and do likewise. This is what I am about. This is the meaning of my life.'

"And then he took his small mirror and, holding it carefully, caught the bright rays of daylight streaming through the window and reflected them onto my face and onto the student's face and hands that were folded on the desk." And he said these words:

- Where there is darkness, let us bring light;

- Where there is despair, let us bring hope;

- Let us walk in the Light of the Lord.

Sometimes we forget that we must be a reflection of God and we must live lives giving the light of a good example to all we meet.

In the Gospel today Jesus talks about a man who is thrown out into the darkness because he is not dressed in the proper garment. When the Bible speaks about a garment it means the deeds we do or the works we accomplish. The man in the Gospel didn't have the good attitude or the works necessary to be at the wedding in the kingdom so he was asked to leave. Sometimes in our lives we need to look at how we are dressed. Are we dressed in the proper works? We need to ask ourselves who have we helped, who have we comforted, who have we encouraged. These are the garments Jesus is talking about.

Take some time today and see what kind of attitude we are clothed in. If we see we are not helping, friendly and tolerant of one another, if not then we must change so we can be a reflection of Jesus. Each time you see a mirror, remember that is you reflecting Jesus.

Trust yourself

Two psychiatrists were at a convention. One said to the other "what was your most difficult case?" The other said once I had a patient who lived in a pure fantasy world, he believed that he had a very rich uncle in South America who was going to leave him a great fortune. All day long he would wait for a make believe letter to arrive from a fictitious attorney. He never would go out or did anything. He just sat around and waited. What was the result asked the other man. Well it was an eight year struggle, but I finally cured him. Then that stupid letter he was waiting for arrived.

This man knew what to do and what would be best for him, but the people around him tried to coax him into their way of thinking. We have the same thing happen to us when we know that we should spend time with Jesus but the things of the world push us to leave Jesus behind. We say to ourselves Jesus will be there later, I will spend time with Him then, and later never comes.

Martha coaxed Mary to come and help with the serving. Was that bad? No. But being with Jesus gives meaning to the things we do in life. When we put Jesus first the things we have to do seem so much easier to do. Martha was in a frenzy doing her work. Just think how much better it would have been for her if she would have left them behind for a few moments and then gone back to them, how much more peaceful she would be. Let me show you how easy it is to put Jesus first.

One day a telemarketer in the office told me that he couldn't get as many appointments as the other telemarketers. I took a few moments and listened to him. I found that he was finishing one call and starting another instantly. He would rush through the call and then make another. I told him to pause for a few moments between calls and relax. To do this I said sit for 30 seconds and say a word like peace, love, or even God if he chose to. When he did this he moved into the next call with ease. He left the anxiety and nervousness behind and was able to give his full attention to the next call.

As he changed the way he made the calls his productivity improved and that changed his attitude from insecure to confident. In the minute we spend relaxing we move into the presence of God and we leave behind what we had been doing. We move into the next thing fresh and able to handle what comes along. In that small piece of time God is able to refresh us and we have a new power to live life with.

The story of Martha and Mary happens in each thing we do in life. You will notice the call of Martha is urgent and usually uses the words hurry up. God owns everything and there is nothing you can give Him that He doesn't own. He owns the shoes on your feet, the clothes on your back, your homes and cars. But there is one thing He doesn't own. And that is your attention. To sit and face God for a moment in silence is the greatest gift you can give Him. Sitting in a moment of silence means you are putting all else you could be doing, even thinking, aside for God, and for that gift He gives you a generous reward, Happiness, peace and success.

Take time in all the things you do today and be like Mary. Place yourself in the presence of God and you will become a different person.

Learn to see beyond

A long time ago there was a man who went on a journey in search of a mystical river he had heard about. It was said that this river had great mystical powers that could heal, cleanse and strengthen a person and once they experienced the river they would have great joy.

When the man found the river, he sat down next to it. He drank from it; he bathed in it and he stayed many days and nights, listening to its mystical teachings. Before he left, he took a picture of the river so he would remember his great experience.

When he returned to his home town his family, friends and townspeople all noticed the joy this man now radiated. He showed them the picture he had taken and as they looked at it asked many questions about his experience. They wanted to know about the teachings he learned and what it was like to be in there. The man told them, "You must go for yourselves and experience the river. You must see, listen, and touch, it for yourselves. I could never fully describe or hope to explain the beauty and mystery I experienced there."

To his surprise the people asked for the picture he took of the river and they put it in a special frame of gold, built a large building and hung the picture on the wall so they could come and gaze at it for hours at a time. Seeing what had happened, the man was saddened. He wished he had never taken that picture of the mystical river because the people didn't understand that the true meaning was to experience the river.

The mystical river in this story is Jesus our teacher. He is the one who loves us, heals us, refreshes us, gives us strength and teaches us how to love. And we sometimes are the people who admire the picture of what he teaches rather than experiencing his teachings and his gifts for ourselves.

The true meaning of Christmas is that our creator came to be with us to show us how to live with each other and to love each other. He didn't overwhelm us with his power but rather he showed us how to be humble and kind towards one another. He wanted us to know that he loved us all equally. And all he required in return was that we accept his gift graciously and experience it to the fullest.

So Christmas is not about the giving of a gift or the receiving of it but it's about the love with which it is given or received. Christmas is a time in which we must experience its true meaning by mending relationships, remembering old friends whom God had sent into our lives and calling them and letting them know how much you appreciate them. This Advent season we should prepare ourselves to receive our greatest gift, Jesus. And we must experience this gift with open hearts and humility.

We must not be like the people in the story who worshiped the picture of the mystical river, but be people who are ready willing and able to experience Jesus our mystical river, who heals us, teaches us and cleanses us. So this Christmas open your heart and allow yourselves to experience the true meaning of Christmas. Experience the beautiful mystical river called Jesus.

Feeling lost or alone

Once there was a very unattractive little girl who lived in an orphanage. The people in charge didn't like her and hoped with all their heart that some long-lost relative would come and claim her. One day one of the staff spotted the little girl writing a note and leaving it tucked in a branch in a tree near the gate; he reported what he saw to the people in charge. They were delighted. They said to each other, could she be at last communicating with a friend, or even a relative. Their hopes soared as they thought of the possibilities. As soon as the little girl was out of sight, they went to the tree, pulled out the wrinkled note, and opened it. There, in the child's handwriting were the words, whoever finds this note, I love you.

When Jesus spoke the Beatitudes to the people today they were like this little girl. They felt alone. They were a group that thought they were not acceptable to God because of the hardships they had to endure. They felt that they were cursed by God rather than loved by Him. But Jesus spoke the Beatitudes to this group of people because he wanted them to know how much God loved them and that they were entitled to share in the kingdom.

Sometimes we feel like this little girl or the group that Jesus was speaking to. So, we need to hear the Beatitudes as they reflect God's love for us in our own time and circumstances and to remember that the Kingdom of God is ours as well.

Picture Jesus coming to this church and that He places a folding chair right in the center isle so He can be one of us. And listen to His words as he would say them to you today:

"If you're struggling to pay the bills, but insist on making time to be with your children whenever they need you, blessed are you   you may never own the big vacation home or a Lexus, but heaven will be yours."

"If you are overwhelmed by the care of a dying spouse, a sick child or an elderly parent but you are determined to make a loving home for them, blessed are you   one day your sorrow will be transformed into joy."

"If you willingly give your time to cook at a soup kitchen, vacuum the church, help in a classroom; if you befriend the unpopular, or the perpetually lost, blessed are you   count God among your friends."

"If you refuse to take shortcuts when it comes to doing what is right, if you refuse to compromise your integrity and ethics, if your refuse to take refuge in the words 'everybody does it,' blessed are you because you will triumph."

"If you try to understand things from the perspective of the other person and always manage to find a way to make things work for the good; if you're feeling discouraged and frustrated because you are always worrying, always waiting, always bending over backwards, always paying the price for loving the unlovable and forgiving the undeserving, blessed are you God will welcome, forgive and love you."

"If you struggle to discover what God asks of you in all things; if you seek God's presence in every facet of your life and every decision you make; if your constant prayer is not 'give me' but 'help me,' blessed are you, because God will always be there for you."

"If you spend time listening and consoling anyone who looks to you for support, for guidance, for compassion; if you manage to heal wounds and build bridges; if others see in you graciousness, joy and serenity; if you can see the good in everyone and seek the good for everyone, blessed are you because you are nothing less than God's own child."

"If you are rejected or demeaned because of the color of your skin or the sound of your name; if your faith automatically puts you at odds with some people; if you refuse to compromise to 'get along' or 'not make waves,' blessed are you   one day you will live with God."

It is in times like these we need to remember the Beatitudes so we may grow in Light, strength, love and peace.

Remember, Jesus says "Rejoice and be glad, you are the blessed of God. In the end, heaven is yours."

Know the Shepherd

There was a poet who just had his works published and he was invited to read them in a group of about 30 people. That night he took selected readings and he began to read to these people. The people smiled and they loved listening to his beautiful voice. After about an hour of reading he was closing the session, the people asked him to read a few more verses. The poet said, what would you have me read.

One of the people in the group said Psalm 23. He thought for a moment and then he said I will do it but only if the gentleman in the back will read Psalm 23 after I do. The poet had pointed to an old priest who was sitting in the back. Well the priest looked a bit puzzled and said, "How can I compare to your reading, my voice is not like your voice. The way I read is not the way you read." But the poet said, "I will only read Psalm 23 if you agree to read after me." The priest reluctantly agreed. He didn't know what good could come out of this.

The poet began "The Lord is my shepherd there's nothing I shall want....." As he continued to read the people began to smile and had pleasant looks on their faces. They were enjoying his reading as they did all the others that night. When he had finished he waited for the priest. The priest got up from his seat walk slowly towards the poet took the book from him and he began to read some Psalm 23. He began "The Lord is my shepherd there's nothing I shall want...." The priest voice was weak, not only was it weak but it cracked and was uneven as he read. As the priest read Psalm 23 something wonderful happened, the people began to have tears come down from their faces. By the time the priest had ended there wasn't a dry eye in the group.

The priest finished then he went back to his seat and the poet said to the people, when I read you enjoyed it. I read and you listened with your ears but when this priest read you cried because he touched your heart. The difference between our readings is that I know the words to the 23rd Psalm but the priest knows the shepherd. Few of us know God, as the priest did. But that is what we are called to do. We are called to love God with all our being and to learn from Him so that we can learn to love, care for and shepherd others. When we have a deep love for God we find it easier to love our brothers and sisters.

Jesus knows each of us as his sheep. He loves us, looks for us when we are lost, strengthens us when we are weak, leads us and bandages are wounds. Each of us has been entrusted with people to watch after as a shepherd. The sheep we have in our lives are our children, our friends and all those that God has brought to us. It takes time, patience and love to be a shepherd. You will watch them get hurt as they make their mistakes and you have to comfort them. They will get lost on the way and it's up to you to help them find the way back to the right road and not abandon them. And most of all you will have to give them forgiveness and encouragement when you feel they don't deserve it.

One day Jesus will judge us based on how good of a shepherd we were to those He entrusted to us. So remember this reading today and place yourself before God once in a while and see how well you are doing.

Ticket master

A friend of mine was telling me about his vacation. He went to Texas by train. On his return it was evening and there was a large crowd of people waiting for the train east. He wondered if they would get a seat even though he knew they only sold enough tickets for the seats that were available. He was wondering if he and his wife would get to sit together. All these worries made him anxious as he waited for the train. Ten minutes before the train was to pull in, the ticket master put on his hat, closed his window and stepped out onto the platform and said: We don't have much time to get all you passengers boarded, so please listen and do as I say. Because if you don't listen you may end up on a car that will be disconnected from the train and attached to another and then you won't get to your destination.

All those with tickets for sleeping compartments stand behind the yellow line you will be in car number one. All those in coach tickets who will be going to New York line up behind the passengers with tickets for the sleeping compartments; you will be in cars two and three. Now those going to Chicago stand by the blue line and so on until all of the destinations were accounted for. My friend began to see that the ticket master had a plan. He knew that if he followed his instructions everything would be OK. So he calmed down. The ticket master concluded with "please get on the train calmly and help those who may need a hand. But remember listen, do as I say and you will reach your destination safely and on time."

As he told me of his experience I began to think how much Jesus had in common with the ticket master. Jesus only wants to get us to our destination safely and on time. And like the ticket master all Jesus asks is that we listen, do as He says and help those who need a hand. These are three simple things we must do, but there are times we don't listen to the ticket master in our lives because we think we know better. He is not going fast enough or we are not where we should be in life. So we may take things into our own hands and begin to move faster. We say how many things can I get done today, how fast can I go. We make ourselves junior ticket masters working on quantity not quality.

Father DeMello told once a story about a man and his wife who were driving across the Midwest and one night he was going 80 miles an hour.

His wife sitting next to him with the map in her hand said dear why are you going so fast you know we are lost. He said I know but we are making great time. In our journey through life we sometimes do the same thing, we go further away from our destination because we think we are making great time but we are getting more lost then before. When we go too fast we go from destination to destination. From home to work, from work to the store from one conversation to another without paying attention to what is going on. Slowing down gives us an awareness of what happens between our destinations and this is just as important the destination itself.

Christmas time is one of those times we can go from destination to destination, going from buying one gift to the next, visiting one person and then another or writing card after card without enjoying the people or appreciating the season and remembering its meaning.

What we need to do is to slow down a little. You know when we slow down we begin to notice the trees and the beauty of creation. We begin to have more meaningful memories. When we slow down we think before we talk and we find peacefulness in doing one thing at a time. Our concentration improves in our work and we become more considerate people. Earnest Hemingway knew the value of proceeding slowly in his work. He would only write 100 words a day, no more; but what words he wrote. In 1954 he was awarded the Pulitzer Prize for Literature.

Going too fast is how we can end up on the wrong car in the train of life. All we have to do to get back on track is to slow down, so we can listen to Jesus and follow the simple things we are responsible for in this reading today.

When he said feed the hungry and give drink to the thirsty it's not only food and drink, in a material sense. It also means can we give encouragement and love to someone and fill them with self-esteem and let them know that we are there for them and that they are important to us. That's real food and drink for the soul. We can welcome a stranger with a warm smile or a hand shake to make them feel that they belong. When we see someone "naked" because of gossip at the office or in our family, we can change the subject and clothe them in their privacy again and restore their dignity. If we see someone ill, depressed or worried. We can give them some of our time and listen to them so they can heal. Is someone you know in prison because of an argument you had. You can release them with a word of forgiveness or apology.

Jesus isn't asking for anything more than the ticket master; just three simple instructions that mean life to us. Listen, do as I say and get on the train of life calmly and help those who need a hand.

Our judgment doesn't happen all at once, it is based on each action we take in our lives, one thing at a time. Each smile we bring out of a person or each frown. When we meet Jesus on Judgment day and he asks us what we did, will we be able to tell him about the journey and the little things, the smile of a child, the beauty of a friendship, or the enjoyment of a warm summer day, or will we only tell him of our destinations and not remember who was there or even why we were there.

If we follow the instructions of our ticket master, Jesus, we will be among the sheep that He will welcome into the heavenly kingdom, our true destination and home. Pray to Jesus today so we can slow down and hear His voice in our lives, that he may guide us home safely.

True treasure

Many years ago there was a farmer who lived with his two sons on their vineyard. All that the farmer ever wanted was for his two sons to become good farmers like himself. Now one day the farmer received news from his doctor that he was dying. The doctor told him he might be able to bring in one more crop before he goes. Realizing that this would be his last crop he wondered how he would show his sons the real value of the vineyard compared to the treasures of the world. The farmer decided to plant more vines and plant them very deep in the soil. When the farmer realized his time was close he called his sons together and he said "boys I'm about to leave this world. I want you to know that all I have is yours and all I have is hidden in the vineyard. You will find everything I have to give you there. The boys thought there was a treasure buried somewhere in the vineyard. They began to picture gold coins and jewels and all different kinds of valuable things. When their father died the boys took their shovels and they dug up every inch of the soil looking for the hidden treasure. Of course there was no hidden treasure as the boys pictured it. The farmer knew that the boys would turn over every inch of the farm looking for the treasure and he also knew that the soil had to be turned over and loosened so the new crop would come through. So when the boys turned the soil over the ground yielded the biggest crop they ever saw. It was then they knew the real treasure their father passed on to them.

Jesus like the farmer is leaving this world in the Gospel reading today and he has left a treasure in the vineyard of our hearts. In the second reading John tells us that the treasure in our hearts is love. Hidden there very deep in our hearts there is enough love for God, ourselves and our neighbors all we have to do is to turn over the soil and soften our hearts and we will be as rich as kings and queens.

A few years ago I worked with a man who was a real aggravating person. He was always demanding and very picky and he always wanted everything done right away. Now I know you don't know anyone like this. Every day when I would go into the office I would have a message on my desk to call him. I would reluctantly pick up the phone and speak with him. He would tell me what he wanted and I for the most part would always give him the bare minimum of what he would ask for. I would make him work hard to request the things he wanted.

After some time I was getting worn-out with the constant aggravation. So one day I decided that I would give him everything he wanted and I would make it easy for him to get. I was amazed at how his attitude changed he was more polite to me and more grateful for the work I was doing for him. When his attitude changed my attitude changed and I began to like working with this person.

I learned that if I softened my heart, love would come out and in turn, the heart of the other person would soften. It's called what you give is what you get. This is something I should have known.

If we begin to treat people with love they will treat us with love. If we treat them with anger they will treat us with anger. The more we are nice to people the more they will be nice to us and that's when life becomes more enjoyable.

Next week is Pentecost and we are reminded that the Holy Spirit is there for us to soften our hearts help us love more deeply and to help us strengthen this love within our families, work place and our church community.

This week marks the end of a journey. It is a time we look back to the commitment we made to God in the beginning of the Lenten season. Have we continued to live and love in a new way or have we gone back to the way we were. In the Christmas season Jesus teaches us how to live, love and enjoy life. He teaches us the true meaning of love of family and neighbor.

In the Lenten season He teaches us how to die to ourselves and the world. But ordinary time it is our time to show God what we have learned. This season is our true test. Ordinary time is not a time to relax but a time to put into practice what we have learned. Today we should take some time and think of what we have learned. Did we learn to love? Do people in our lives treat us well? If not we need to look at the image we project because remember what you give is what you get. There is still time to change. There is still time to love.

Jesus prays for us today in the Gospel and we should join our prayers to His so that we will be strengthened to continue our journey and become good farmers of the heart cultivating love and reaping the treasure Jesus placed in our hearts.

Renew yourself and others

One day Queen Victoria paid a visit to a paper mill. Without knowing who this distinguished visitor was, the foreman showed her the workings of the mill. Along the way the Queen went into the rag-sorting shop where employees picked out the rags from the garbage of the city. The Queen asked the foreman what they were going to do with the pile of dirty rags. He told her that those dirty rags would go through a process that would eventually transform them into the finest white writing paper. After she left, the foreman was surprised to find out that it was the Queen who had paid a visit to the mill. So some time later, Her Majesty received a package from the foreman of the most delicate, pure white stationery, bearing her likeness for a watermark. Enclosed was a note saying that the stationery had been made from the dirty rags she had recently inspected.

This story illustrates how God works in us and makes us into new creatures. In that transformation we become a page in history ready for God to continue writing his book of the human journey giving encouragement and love to those who read it.

A few years ago I was talking to a friend of mine and I told him that it was hard for me to understand the Trinity. He told me that the way he understood the mystery of the Trinity was through something that happened to him a long time ago. He said that when he was younger he lost his job and couldn't find work for quite a while. He said he realized he wasn't living the best life and that he had done many things he wasn't proud of and that he had become very bitter. Then one day a friend of his found out about his problem and offered him a job so he could get back on his feet. It wasn't much of a job, but he was back to work. He said he noticed that on the job people began to encourage him and to help him. He said for the first time in a long time he felt a part of something good, he felt needed, respected and loved.

As time went on he began to feel a motion within him that made him content and peaceful. He began to help others and encourage them in their work. He said that today he has surpassed the position he held years ago and that he has become a productive good citizen. He said it was the Trinity that was there for him and transformed him. The Father who gives life opened the heart of his friend to get him a job. Jesus then began to work through the people around him to make him feel loved. And the Holy Spirit made him come alive inside by giving him light to see how to live and share his new life with others. It was then that I understood that the Father will always introduce us to new life and new circumstances by bringing others into our lives and Jesus will be there to encourage and love us. The Spirit will open our minds and hearts to see and we will gain the courage and strength to grow and move forward.

No matter what your condition in life if you open your heart to the Trinity you will have new life, love and light to transform you into that new page in history that others will look at, and they will find in you the comfort of God's presence so that they too can be transformed.

Seeing with your heart

There were two men in a hospital room. The man by the window was allowed to sit up in his bed for an hour each afternoon to help drain the fluid from his lungs. The man in the bed next to him had to spend all his time flat on his back. The two men would speak for hours. They spoke of their wives and families, their homes, their jobs, even where they had been on vacation. Every afternoon when the man in the bed by the window would sit up and he would pass the time by describing to his roommate all the things he saw outside the window. The other man, who wasn't allowed to move from his bed, began to live for those one-hour periods where his roommate would describe what he saw outside the window. His world would be broadened and enlivened by all the activity and color of the world outside. The man by the window described a park with a lovely lake. Ducks and swans played on the water, while children sailed their model boats. Young lovers walked arm in arm amidst flowers of every color of the rainbow. Grand old trees graced the landscape, and a view of the city skyline could be seen in the distance. As the man by the window described all this in perfect detail, the man on the other side of the room would close his eyes and imagine the picturesque scene. One warm afternoon the man by the window described a parade that was passing by. Although the other man couldn't hear the band, he could see it in his mind's eye as the man by the window used such beautifully descriptive words. Days and weeks passed with this great happiness, and then one morning, the man in the bed by the window died.

After a few days the other man asked if he could be moved next to the window. The nurse was happy to make the switch, and after making sure he was comfortable, she left him alone. Slowly, painfully, he propped himself up on one elbow to take his first look at the world outside. He turned his head towards the window to see the beautiful park for the first time but all he saw was the wall of the building next door. There was no park or pond or no ducks, and no people, just a wall. When the nurse returned the man said to the nurse, "What could have made my roommate describe such wonderful things outside this window." The nurse smiled and said, "That the man who passed away was blind, he wasn't even able to see the wall of the next building. What he described to you was seen with his heart not his eyes."

Most of our lives we see only with our eyes not with our hearts. But I will tell you this if you really want to live, and if you really want to love, you must look at things with your heart not with your eyes.

A few weeks ago I was at one of the first Holy Communion services. I watched the children march in and take their places. They sang a song, shared the readings. With my eyes I saw children. But when I opened my heart I saw the children as they could be. I saw them as parents, and teachers. I saw a doctor or two and a business owner. I saw in these children our future. But I couldn't see this until I looked at them with my heart. Just like the blind man in the bed who looked at the wall and saw the beauty of creation in his heart I saw the beauty of God's work in these children.

This is what today all about. It's seeing with our hearts and not our eyes. When we come to mass we see a piece of bread with our eyes but when we open our hearts we see Jesus. Seeing with the heart is very important. If an artist doesn't see with his heart his canvas would be blank. If we don't look at life with our hearts we may never know what we can be. We have to be like the blind man today and open our hearts if we are to see God in our lives and the beauty in each other.

I invite you to take some time today and sit quiet and allow your heart to open and begin to look at your lives through your hearts. You will be surprised at the beautiful things you will see.

Choosing between health, success and love

One day a woman was looking out her front window and she saw three men coming toward her house. They had long gray beards and they looked tired and hungry. The woman called her husband and daughter to the window and asked if she should invite them in to have something to eat? The three of them agreed and the wife said "I will go and invite them in to be our guests!"

The woman went out and said to the three men, "My family and I would like you to come in for something to eat, and to rest for a while. Please be our guests." "You can only choose one of us to be your guest." they replied. "Why is that?" The woman wanted to know. One of the old men explained this fellow's name is Wealth, the other man's name is Success and my name is Love. It's up to you which one of us you invite into your home. Please go and decide, with your family which one of us you have chosen to be your guest.

Well the woman went in and told her husband and daughter what they said and her husband was overjoyed. "How nice!" he said. "Since that is the case, let's invite Wealth to be our guest. Then our home will be filled with wealth! We will have new cars and money and all of the things we ever wanted. How happy we will be. His wife strongly disagreed. "My dear, why don't we invite Success? Then all that we do will come out right. Could you imagine anything we do will be the right thing, even my cooking will come out perfect." Their daughter saw what was happening. She jumped in with her own suggestion: "I think it would be better to invite Love to be in our home. Our home will then be filled with love and care!" They thought about it for a moment and said, "She is right let's take our daughter's advice." The husband said to his wife, "Go out and invite Love to be our guest."

The woman went out and asked the 3 old men, "Which one of you is Love?" Please come in and be our guest." Love got up and started walking toward the house. The other 2 men also got up and followed him. Surprised, the lady said to Wealth and Success: "I only invited Love, Why are you coming in? "The old men replied together: "If you had invited Wealth or Success, the other two of us would've stayed out, but since you invited Love, wherever he goes we go with him.

When we have love, all of the things we already have in life become wealth. The home we thought was too small now has enough room. The car we have with the slightly dull paint becomes shiny with character and memories. When we have love, the smallest things we do are always successful. Like the dinner we cook, the home we fix, or the conversation we have with our children, these become our greatest successes in life. Love gives meaning to ordinary objects, talents and relationships.

Years ago I had a friend who worked for the lottery commission and it was his responsibility at that time to do a review of what had happened to the lottery winners in the first two years of drawings. He found that almost all of the winners had lost friends and family over the newfound wealth.

One of the stories he told me was about two friends that had been together for 40 years; went their separate ways in anger. If only they had love, then the wealth could have been shared.

As we stand before a new day you have a choice to make. Will you be looking through the eyes of love or through the eyes of wealth or success? Today that choice is yours. Please choose wisely. Please choose love.

Be a team player

A well known organist was performing a concert on the huge, antique organ in the local church. The bellows were hand pumped by a boy who was behind the screen, unseen by the audience. The first part of the performance was well received. The audience was thrilled by the organist's ability at the keyboard of the old instrument. After taking his bows and accepting the ovation, the musician walked triumphantly into a side passageway. As he passed the boy he heard him say, "We played well, didn't we sir?" The organist looked down at the boy and said, "And what do you mean, 'we'?"

After the intermission, the organist returned to his seat at the impressive five keyboard console and began to play. But nothing happened, not a sound was heard. Then the organist heard the young boy's voice whisper from behind the screen, "Say, mister, now do you know what "we" means?"

All of us are like the organist at times, especially when we master a new work in our lives, or get something we want. We forget who we called on for help.

When we first take a job we are worried if we will do well or if we will be accepted and we frequently speak with God looking for his help and encouragement. Then time goes by and we feel more confident and we speak less frequently with God. Soon, we stop speaking to him at all because we feel we have things in control the way we want. We even begin to think that God had nothing to do with it at all. This happens to us when we fall in love as well, we pray to God to help us find someone and when we get them we never again treat them with the respect we should. We forget they were a gift from God. We want to have children so we pray to God to help us to have them and when we get them we don't pay attention to them. Again God is nowhere to be found.

In the Gospel today Jesus asks the Father to allow us to be one with Him and to share in that mysterious, unseen, and often unexpected force that transforms the ordinary world we live in into something wonderful. He asks that we share in the spirit that forges strong and lasting friendships between individuals; it is the spirit that transforms a group of people into a community of faith and family. This union in the spirit Jesus wants for us enables us, to recreate our world in the love of God. It is in the Spirit that we are connected to God.

So don't be like the organist that had to hear the words "Do you know what we means now?" Rather be a person who always remembers that God is a partner in your life and that he wants to live every moment with you; both in good times and bad. And never think so much of yourselves that you forget that it is He who breathes the breath of success into all that you do and gives you all that you have. So acknowledge God's presence in your lives and you will find peace, love, joy, and friendship.

Have one target

A wise old archer was training two young warriors. Across the meadow was a small target hanging from a tree. The first warrior took an arrow from his quiver, readied it in his bow, and took aim. The old archer asked him to describe everything he saw. "I see the sky, the clouds, the trees, and leaves, the branches and the target," he answered. "Put your bow down," the old archer said. "You are not ready." The second warrior stepped up and readied his bow with an arrow. The old man ordered him, "Describe everything you see." "There is only the target," he said. "Then, shoot!" was the command. The arrow flew straight and hit the target. "Very good," said the old archer. "When you see only the target, your aim will be true, and your arrows will fly according to your wish." It seems that the first archer had too many things in his sight to hit the target.

We are like the young warriors in the story and God is the wise old archer who is training us to concentrate on the target we call goodness. Each day in our lives we have our work to do, and we have friendships to work at. But it's not easy because the evil is always there to distract us and to give us false targets that only look good but are not of benefit to anyone.

The other day I had to go to a meeting that lasted four hours. My assignment was to get 12 people that owned their own businesses, to agree to do one small piece of work together. As the meeting progressed the people started to all go in different directions. Everyone had to say their piece. Some began to complain about what had to be done and that they don't have the time to do it. Then they began to complain about each other. One person said about another "he doesn't listen to me." Finally they complained about themselves and how inadequate they were for the job we had to do. They couldn't see their target; goodness! These people were like the warrior having too many targets and their arrows were going in different directions.

I needed to bring them to look at the target. I began to make a list with them of all the good things that could come out of their work.

I asked questions like:

- Does this project help the people we are serving?
- Can this project make available a healing process for others?
- Will people be more educated so they can do a better job?
- As a result will they be able to support their families better?

Soon, they were all hitting the target. And the target was the good that would come out of the work they were doing. Whenever you bring into a conversation the good it will produce you are hitting the mark.

In the Gospel today Jesus says forget everything in your life that others taught you. Remember only this; our purpose is to do good things and to give freedom and peace to others by the good work we do. Today when you speak to each other, speak only of good and uplifting things and you will be hitting your mark. When you do some small work today before you begin to do it think of all the good that will come out of this work, then you will be hitting your mark. I ask you to pray to God today that you be good marksmen and Jesus will show you the target.

Remember your destination

Supreme court Justice Oliver Wendell Holmes had the reputation of being absent minded. One day on a train out of Washington, he was studying a pending case when the conductor asked for his ticket. Mr. Holmes searched every pocket nervously, but couldn't find his ticket. Don't worry, Justice Holmes the conductor said, we know who you are. When you return to Washington you can send us the ticket at your convenience. Holmes lowered his eyes and shook his head sadly. "Thank you he said to the conductor, but you don't seem to understand the problem. It's not the question of whether I will pay the fare. The problem is; where am I going?"

Every once in a while because we are so busy we get absent-minded and we forget our purpose and destination in this life. God in His goodness touches our hearts to remind us of what we are about.

Last week in the outreach section of the bulletin there was a story of a man who, like Justice Holmes became absent-minded, and God reminded him of his purpose in a most unusual way. This man came to the outreach one Saturday morning in a van with his two sons. I opened the door and he proceeded to unload seventeen bags of toys. Then, when he was done he handed me an envelope with two thousand dollars in cash in it for families who might be having a difficult time this Christmas. When I asked him how he became to be so generous and he told me that years ago he was watching television and he saw a cartoon character called Alf. In one of the episodes Alf visited a children's ward in a hospital and Alf was giving gifts to the children and this man noticed the smile on the children's faces and from that moment on he promised himself that he would do the same. His enlightening moment happened back in 1987 and his life has never been the same.

An epiphany is an awakening of the mind and heart to God's way. And it is a journey in which we find wisdom, understanding, meaning, and purpose. It is an adventure, in which we confront the "giants" real and imaginary that keep us from making our way to God.

The Gospel of the Epiphany challenges us to slow down and check our bearings, and focus on the "star" that point to Jesus. When we do, we make our lives what God has created them to be, by fixing our eyes on the constant, eternal values of peace, compassion, mercy, justice, forgiveness and generosity that are of God.

Erasing the darkness

Years ago there were no electric street lights in the city, kerosene lamps were used to light the streets. They had a man, called a lamplighter, who had a candle attached to a long pole and when darkness would come he would go to the end of the street and he begin lighting all of the kerosene lamps along the way. From a distance you couldn't see the lamplighter very well because the light from one small candle wasn't bright enough to take away the darkness of the night. However, you could follow the progress of the lamplighter as he went along the street.

With each lamp he lit, the glow would erase a portion of the darkness. Looking back down the street, you could see that the light from the glowing street lamps made the entire street bright. The darkness was no more because of the lamplighter.

Today in the gospel Jesus meets two disciples and he hands them the light of faith. Those disciples have handed down the light of faith to us and it is our responsibility to hand this light of faith to future generations. But the flame of faith is only passed on through the quality of good character. Good character is defined as having moral excellence that causes a person to do the right thing, which comes to life through right and proper actions even when the internal or external pressures are against them.

There have been many who have gone before us that have passed on this precious light of faith to us. Mother Theresa by her determination to do the right thing changed the world when she went to Calcutta and fed the poorest of the poor. By her action and good character she has passed on the light of faith through compassion to the world. John Paul the II was shot in St. Peter's Square on May 13th 1981, and when he recovered he forgave the man who shot him. John Paul passed on the light of faith by his good character to forgive. Father Tom our pastor was a man of good character and he through appropriate actions handed on the light of faith to this parish as to how to love and serve his people.

Good character is the thing inside you that makes you stand up for the rights of those who cannot speak for themselves. Good character is the quality that makes you have courtesy and respect for others. Good character is the quality that sums up the teaching in the scriptures.

Without people of good character our faith will cease to be. We must not let this happen. We must follow the example of Jesus, who is our light, and remember that by his example he changed a dark cold world into a place of hope with endless possibilities for us.

So today we must be determined to be people of good character so that we may pass on the light of faith to the next generation by our good actions and perseverance.

Pointing the way

A few years ago one of the schools had a Christmas pageant and there was a little girl by the name of Kaitlin. Now Kaitlin had a part but she didn't tell her father what the part was. Kaitlin's father thought she must have had one of the main parts because of how excited she was that morning.

The parents were all there and one by one the children took their places. The shepherds were fidgeting in the corner. Mary and Joseph stood solemnly behind the manger. In the back you could see three young wise men waiting impatiently. And at the edge of the stage little Kaitlin sat quietly and confidently. Then the teacher began: "A long time ago Mary and Joseph had a baby and they called him Jesus. And when Jesus was born a bright star appeared over the stable"

At that cue Kaitlin got up and picked up a large tinfoil star walked behind Mary and Joseph and held the star up for everyone to see. When the teacher spoke of the shepherds coming to see the baby, Kaitlin jiggled the star up and down excitedly for the shepherds to show them where to come. When it was time for the wise men to come in Kaitlin went forward to meet them and to lead the way. Kaitlin had such a big smile on her face as she did her part.

The play ended and as Kaitlin and her family were on the way home she said with great satisfaction "I had the main part" Her father said you did, wondering why she thought that. "Yes" she said, "'cause I showed everybody how to find Jesus". How true the words Kaitlin spoke in that moment to her father, to show others how to find Jesus and to be the light for their paths that is the finest roll we can play in life.

Each of us is called in life to be a guiding light to another person. Just like Kaitlin held the star over the holy family so that the shepherds and the kings could find Jesus so must we do the same for others. It's not easy to be a guiding light to another person, or a profit, it takes time, strength and patience.

It's Christmas and it's time to show the light of Christ to others. The way we do that is by our actions. As parents we show the light of Jesus to our children when we love them the way Jesus loved children. He hugged them and blessed them; He was their friend and example. He followed the same rules that he gave to others to follow. He didn't think of himself as special. As we practice our skills in the work place we must be a profit by showing people that we work hard and follow the rules of courtesy and respect for each other.

We also need to show the people in our lives how much we appreciate them and need them to be with us. We don't need to show them by a gift, but by spending a little time with them, and telling them how much we love them and have enjoyed their good and precious qualities. In this day and age it is not easy to show appreciation and love to others. But it can be done by taking the first step and doing something small and by doing this we can change the world.

Acknowledgments

I am grateful to Twenty-Third Publications and The Paulist Press for allowing me permission to use several of their stories as a foundation for some of the examples I have used in this book.

From the Paulist Press:

Excerpts from Sower's Seeds Aplenty, Fourth Planting, by Brian Cavanaugh, T.O.R.. Copyright © 1996 by Brian Cavanaugh, T.O.R.. Paulist Press, Inc., New York/Mahwah, NJ. Reprinted by permission of Paulist Press, Inc. www.paulistpress.com

Excerpts from More Sower's Seeds, Second Planting, by Brian Cavanaugh, T.O.R.. Copyright © 1992 by Brian Cavanaugh, T.O.R.. Paulist Press, Inc., New York/Mahwah, NJ. Reprinted by permission of Paulist Press, Inc. www.paulistpress.com

Excerpts from Fresh Packet of Sower's Seeds, Third Planting, by Brian Cavanaugh, T.O.R.. Copyright © 1994 by Brian Cavanaugh, T.O.R.. Paulist Press, Inc., New York/Mahwah, NJ. Reprinted by permission of Paulist Press, Inc. www.paulistpress.com

Excerpts from Sower's Seeds of Encouragement, Fifth Planting, by Brian Cavanaugh, T.O.R.. Copyright © 1998 by Brian Cavanaugh, T.O.R.. Paulist Press, Inc., New York/Mahwah, NJ. Reprinted by permission of Paulist Press, Inc. www.paulistpress.com

Excerpts from The Sower's Seeds, by Brian Cavanaugh, T.O.R.. Copyright © 2004 by Brian Cavanaugh, T.O.R.. Paulist Press, Inc., New York/Mahwah, NJ. Reprinted by permission of Paulist Press, Inc. www. paulistpress.com

From Twenty-Third Publications:

Excerpts from A World Of Stories For Preachers And Teachers, By William J. Bausch, Copyright © 1998.

Printed in the United States
212136BV00001B/4/P